Finding Your Wings

Finding Your Wings

A WORKBOOK FOR BEGINNING BIRD WATCHERS

BURTON GUTTMAN

HOUGHTON MIFFLIN COMPANY

BOSTON • NEW YORK

2008

Library of Congress Cataloging-in-Publication Data

Guttman, Burton S.
    Finding your wings : a workbook for beginning bird watchers /
Burton Guttman.
        p. cm.
    Includes bibliographical references.
    ISBN-13: 978-0-618-78216-1 (pbk.)
    ISBN-10: 0-618-78216-8 (pbk.)
    1. Bird watching. I. Title.
    QL677.5.G88 2008
    598.072'34—dc22   2007032481

Book design by Anne Chalmers
Typefaces: Minion, DIN

Printed in China

C&C 10 9 8 7 6 5 4 3 2 1

All illustrations except for the following copyright © by Roger Tory Peterson
    Pages 12, 13: Copyright © 1969 from *Perception and Discovery* by Norwood Russell Hanson. (Freeman,
        Cooper, and Co., 1969.) Used by permission of Frances Fay Hanson.
    Pages 24, 25: Burton Guttman
    Page 57 bottom: by Noah Strycker copyright © 2008 by Houghton Mifflin Company. Adapted with per-
        mission of the National Geographic Society from the *Field Guide to the Birds of North America,* 5th ed.
    Pages 62, 107: by Noah Strycker copyright © 2008 by Houghton Mifflin Company.
    Page 65: Copyright © 2002 from *Birding Basics* by David Sibley. Knopf. Used by permission.
    Page 79: Anne Chalmers
    Page 97: Copyright © 1994 from *A Birder's Guide to Eastern Massachusetts* by Bird Observer. American
        Birding Association, Inc.
    Page 130 top: Copyright © 1995 from *Ornithology,* 2nd ed. by Frank B. Gill. Used by permission of
        W. H. Freeman and Company/Worth Publishers.
    Pages 130 bottom, 131 top, 135: Illustrations by Jim Erckmann from *Shorebirds of the Pacific Northwest*
        by Dennis Paulson (1993), University of Washington Press.

Contents

PART II: SOME PROBLEMATIC GROUPS

List of Activities

This workbook consists of four types of activities. Many of the **exercises** require you to refer to either the *Peterson Field Guide to Birds of Eastern and Central North America,* fifth edition, or the *Peterson Field Guide to Western Birds,* third edition. Space is provided to write down your answers, and answers are supplied in the appendix on page 167. **Field exercises** suggest specific observations to make when you're out birding. These will give you substantial practice and improve your birding skills. You will want to make notes on these observations in your field notebook, but no answers are given here, as individual observations will vary. After you complete the written exercises and field exercises, the **quizzes** provide a way to test yourself and make sure you are learning. Finally, the **games** in the last chapter are a fun way to put to use your new knowledge, either on your own or with family members and friends.

Preface

"How do I get started in birding?" Many people ask this question, usually those who have already started to watch birds casually, perhaps at their feeders, but who feel the need for guidance in going further. People at this stage often know some common birds but seem daunted by the prospect of learning to recognize the hundreds of birds shown in their field guides, especially when so many of them look so much alike, and the information for separating one from another seems complicated. This book is one answer to the question.

Birding, or bird watching, is becoming more and more popular as a pastime. New field guides to the birds of North America try to make identification easier, and other books offer advice to novices about moving beyond the casual enjoyment of birds and starting to develop some expertise. But I believe these books, for all their excellent information and advice, fall short of what beginners need; they assume that beginners with minimal skills can jump into the middle of an often complicated activity whose skills take a long time to develop. In this book I've taken a different approach by trying to figure out what beginners need to know first and what skills they need to acquire first, and then guiding them, step by step, through those ideas.

For several years, I've taken beginners on winter walks around the lakes and waterfront in Olympia, Washington; we focus on the water birds, especially the ducks. It is much easier to observe and identify ducks than to see tiny songbirds scurrying through leafed-out bushes and trees in the spring and summer. I introduce the two primary lessons that I think beginners need: how to *see* the features of birds, and how to divide the huge world of species into *categories* that observers can recognize and use to identify a bird to a species within a category. Although participants find these introductions useful, they are very limited, of course. As a more extended exercise for beginners, I have collaborated with Tom Schooley, a knowledgeable local birder, to conduct a Birding 101 course for the Black Hills Audubon Society, with four or five evening sessions and a few field trips. Participants have expressed a lot of satisfaction with these classes and have asked us to go further.

I introduce Birding 101 by telling participants that a lifetime of college teaching has taught me an important lesson about teaching in general: *I can't do it.* I then hasten to explain that that doesn't mean I'm a lousy teacher; my portfolio of evaluations by students tells me that, on the whole, I've done very well in helping students learn science and other subjects. No, I mean I'm convinced that the verb *to teach* is not as active or meaningful as the verb *to learn*. A fundamental truth about education is that no one can really teach you anything; you learn only what you do for yourself in an active, involved way. A teacher can encourage a child to learn the multiplication table. She can provide incentives, strategies, practice, perhaps some helpful mnemonic devices, and tests to see if the child is learning, but she can't open the child's skull and pour the learning in. Similarly, I can help you learn about birds by providing basic instruction and some advice about strategies and points to pay attention to, but you will learn best by doing the workbook exercises and by going out into the field and spending long, enjoyable hours actually observing birds and perhaps struggling to identify them. The birding maven Pete Dunne in his book *Pete Dunne on Bird Watching* writes, "Don't go into the field with an open mind," and he gives some general advice about how to prepare your mind. That's what this book is for — preparing your mind to go out into the field to observe. If you aspire to go beyond the pleasures of casually enjoying the beauty of birds and their songs, I'm convinced it is useless, even counterproductive, to go out and watch birds naively, without some kind of preparation as to *how to see* and *what to look for*. This book provides that preparation, point by point. You can study the book at your leisure and take it at your own pace. You don't need me looking over your shoulder to see if you've got the right answers to the questions.

Acknowledgments

I am deeply grateful to Ann Berry, Michael Donahue, David Gascoigne, Erica Guttman, Dave Jackson, and Dave Rintoul, who read the book manuscript and gave me suggestions and corrections that improved it enormously and kept me from embarrassing myself with silly mistakes. I owe special thanks to Kevin Breault, Tom Foote, Todd Newberry, and Dave Milne, who provided especially detailed notes and ideas for improvement. Problems that got into print are the result of my not being smart enough to take everyone's advice.

Among the Houghton Mifflin staff, my gratitude goes first to my editor, Lisa White, for having picked up the project in the first place and then for guiding it to completion with superb intelligence and the perfect blend of grace, sympathy, patience, good humor, and literary discipline. I thank Anne Chalmers for designing a beautiful book; my copyeditor, Tracy Resnik Roe, for keeping my prose to a high standard; and my production editor, Shelley Berg, for seeing the project through all the hurdles to an excellent product. Mimi Assad—who also suggested the book's title—and Clare O'Keeffe handled a variety of details along the way. I am also grateful to Taryn Roeder for her excellent hard work on publicity.

How to Use This Book

This book supplements the field guides by Roger Tory Peterson *A Field Guide to the Birds of Eastern and Central North America*, fifth edition, and *A Field Guide to Western Birds*, third edition. Peterson created a revolution in 1934 with his first book, which was responsible for the modern surge in birding. Before his time, there were a few small guides to common birds, but the most serious identification guides assumed you could examine the plumage of the bird in hand. Peterson showed that an observer in the field could learn to identify birds by using distinctive key features — *field marks,* such as a stripe on the face, the color of the breast, or white tail feathers. His plates show similar birds in identical poses, with arrows pointing out the field marks. Though several excellent field guides to North American birds are now available, none is better for beginners. This book is essentially an extended commentary on the Peterson system. It assumes you have at least one of the books in hand, either the eastern or western guide, and there are references throughout the book to pages, plates, and maps in them, using *E* for pages in the eastern guide and *W* for the western guide. (The latest editions have enormous advantages over earlier ones, especially their newer and more refined range maps that show where each species is to be expected.)

This is a workbook. It contains specific questions and exercises, requiring you to look at certain points in the field guides or to go out and make certain observations. As I explain in chapter 2, birding is largely about learning to see (and to hear), so most of the exercises ask you to look at the birds on a certain plate in the book and see something specific about them. But generally I don't tell you precisely what to look for because I'm trying to force you to *see for yourself,* using your own good eyes and Peterson's expert guidance in the form of arrows and notes. Please use the workbook as it is designed by *writing* your answers to the questions. *Don't just think them.* The act of writing, of *doing* something, is an important aspect of learning. Remember, we learn by actually doing things. If you're unsure of your answers, check mine in the back of the book. And if you're worried about making mistakes, I offer you some words in chapter 1 about the importance of making mistakes.

Even though it's important for you to do this work to develop your personal skills, it can be helpful to share this experience with at least one partner, a close friend who is at about the same level of birding skill. Besides having fun together, you can support and act as sounding boards for each other. Going out in the field together for birding can help you both learn to observe and identify new species. This book is based on the workshop model that my colleagues and I use extensively in formal courses, in which we pose problems and questions for groups of students to discuss. They learn through their active involvement with the ideas, and those who understand best can help those who are having trouble, so the slower students get help and those who take on a teaching role solidify their understanding by having to formulate the concepts carefully and explain them. In a mini-version of such a workshop format, friends can help one another by doing the exercises together. Ideally, you each should have your own copy of the workbook to write your answers in.

THE THREEFOLD PATH

My experience tells me that beginners need to work toward three goals more or less at one time: First, to learn to see as a birder sees, developing the proper "spectacles behind the eyeballs" through which birders perceive the world. Second, to learn about categories of birds, both formal and informal. And third, to learn as many of the easily identified, common local birds as you can.

THE BIRD-BY-BIRD STRATEGY

Anne Lamott named her wonderful little book about writing, *Bird by Bird,* after a family incident. Her brother had to write a paper for school about birds, and he was groaning over the task at the last minute, "surrounded by binder paper and pencils and unopened books on birds, immobilized by the hugeness of the task ahead." Then his father advised him, "Bird by bird, buddy. Just take it bird by bird." That will be one of our strategies, too. Leafing through a field guide, you may feel overwhelmed by the sheer number of species, many of them looking so much alike. So the first thing to do is *relax*. You aren't going to see all those birds right away! They don't all live in the same places, and you aren't going to see many of them at one time. Let me take you figuratively by the hand and lead you bird by bird from one group of birds and one habitat to another, from one species to another. I'll show you how to see specific details of form and behavior that will separate one species from another and how you can learn groups of birds that are easy to recognize.

The Talmud, the book of Jewish tradition and law, says, "All beginnings are hard," and beginning birding may be hard, too. But let me suggest that a relaxed and upbeat attitude can make life easier. When you go out and start to observe, perhaps you can't get everything right immediately and you start to get frustrated. But why get frustrated? Here you are on a pleasant day (well, okay, maybe it's raining, but so what?), walking beside a lovely lake or enjoying a quiet woodland, with beautiful and interesting birds all around you, probably with a variety of beautiful plants, too. Butterflies may be fluttering all around. You don't have to rush to get anywhere right now. You can relax and enjoy your surroundings. And if you can't put a name to every bird, that doesn't really hurt you, does it? No one, not even the most experienced birder, can name everything that flies by. Don't worry about it. Relax and enjoy life.

Enjoy the book, too.

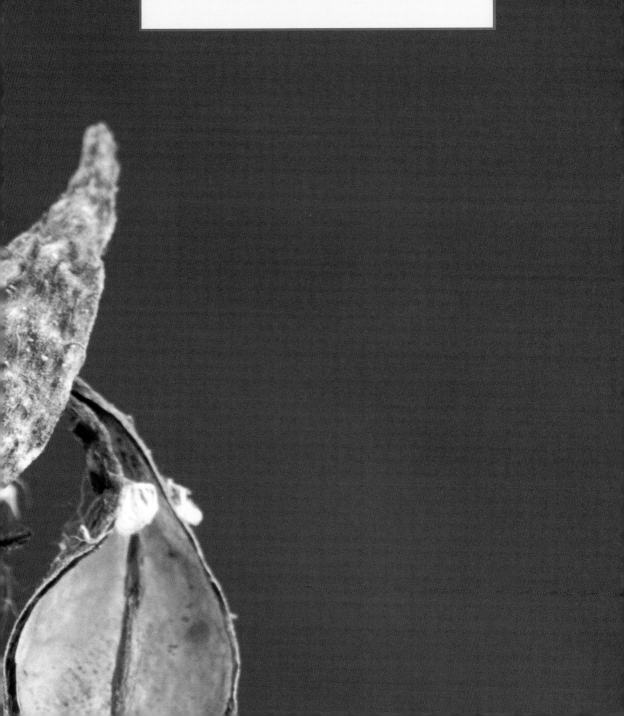

PART I

Basic Principles and Skills

CHAPTER 1

Getting Started

Many words, some eloquent, have been written about why people enjoy watching birds, keeping lists of the birds they've seen, driving long distances to see rare birds, and striving to improve their bird-identification skills. To some, birds symbolize freedom, the ability to take wing easily, fly to great heights, and travel great distances without human encumbrances. Others enjoy birds for their beauty and grace. For most of us, birds are simply the most obvious, most accessible animals on earth, and it takes little effort to see them, admire their beauty, drink in the scene of a tree or a mud flat hosting an array of bright, colorful little creatures. So we crave the pure aesthetic experience, just as we crave and enjoy the pleasure of a Mozart string quartet, an evening with a fine jazz group, or the changing sky at sunset.

The verb *to bird* has now become common, as in "I'm going birding this morning" or "My husband and I birded the Oregon coast yesterday." Is birding different from bird watching? Some disparage bird watching as old-fashioned. Others proudly proclaim themselves *bird watchers* rather than *birders* because they set a leisurely pace for themselves and observe birds carefully for long times, focusing on behavior and recording the birds' activities. *Birding* may imply a more sportslike activity, more rapid paced, more competitive, perhaps more driven by the lure of the list — that is, the determination to see as many different species of birds as possible. In this book, I'll treat *bird watching* and *birding* as synonymous.

Birding — and nature activities in general — offers a special, ineffable pleasure that calls up the words *peace, tranquillity, silence.* The natural world in which we immerse ourselves while birding is a fundamentally tranquil world. (We'll ignore the moment when a crow seizes a frantically screaming nestling robin or an eagle flies down into the jungle to capture and consume a monkey.) I would like to have some remote monitor for measuring the blood pressure of people as they are birding to compare with their usual blood pressure; I'm sure that while people are in the field, their numbers are lower, that their endorphins are flowing well, that digestive systems that otherwise need pampering are more at rest. Particularly in the insane, high-pressure, fast-moving world our society has created, birding offers a wonderfully healthful, restful escape. And for many people, birding and other nature activities have a strongly spiritual, even religious, aspect that becomes an important part of their lives.

Birding also appeals to the collector's instinct. Many birders keep a *life list,* a list of all the species they have identified with certainty. Adding to your life list can become a collector's passion. You might become a more extreme lister, with a list for every state, every county in your state, and you may start a new list every January 1, every year trying to beat the list of last year.

Birding always begins with aesthetic experience, with simple enjoyment of a bird and its surroundings. But it's natural to wonder right away, "What is it?" and so the question of identification arises. That's the purpose of the field guides, of course, and also the focus of the exercises in this book. But the pleasures of watching birds extend to truly watching them, to observing their behavior. Just seeing a pair of adults flying back and forth to their nest with food for their young becomes entrancing. I once watched two little juncos frantically searching for food to stuff into the mouth of a much larger young bird, a cowbird they had been tricked into raising. One morning in Santa Barbara, my daughter and I enjoyed a long bout between a mockingbird and a huge dragonfly it was trying to kill and eat. Every birder has endless stories about the fascination of seeing birds in action, and many books on the subject are available as aids to understanding their behavior.

You've almost surely started birding a little. You've probably been watching the common birds around your home, maybe at a feeder, and you have the ordinary adult's knowledge of different kinds of birds in a general sense — ducks, chickens, geese, crows, and so on. So where do we go from here?

WHAT SHOULD I DO FIRST?

A good way to start is to take care of five items: get good binoculars, get a good field guide, buy a notebook, find a comfortable place to start watching, and start reading.

Binoculars

For most birding you need a good pair of binoculars (*bins* or *binocs,* in birding jargon), though I will argue later that certain pleasures can come from watching birds in quiet, intimate situations without binoculars. Fortunately, binocular optics have advanced so much in recent years that you can get very satisfactory glasses at quite reasonable prices. So please turn to appendix 2, consider what you're able to spend, and buy a good pair.

Field Guides

Get at least one of the Peterson Field Guides. As you become more advanced you'll want to buy other field guides to North American birds. Kenn Kaufman's *Kaufman Field Guide to Birds of North America* is similar to the Peterson Guides but uses edited photographs instead of paintings. Many birders swear by the *National Geographic Field Guide to the Birds of North America*, which covers the entire continent. David Sibley's popular field guides provide an enormous amount of valuable detail and are first-rate for experienced birders. His single large book is good for study at home, and there are separate eastern and western guides to put in your pocket or backpack.

Notebook

Buy a good notebook and develop the habit of writing in it. Buy one that's small enough to fit conveniently in a backpack, but with pages sewn in — not loose-leaf — so they're not easily lost. A notebook with blank pages or graph paper may help you make small sketches of the birds you observe. (See chapter 2 for some notes about making simple drawings of birds.) Take it out in the field and use it as a study aid as you go through this book and other books about birds and birding. Make it a personal tool. This book will help you learn what kinds of notes are most valuable, but it's your book, and you should feel free to write what you please. Record your observations of birds that are new or puzzling to you, to help you identify them or learn them better. Record any interesting bird behavior you observe. Record where you locate each kind of bird, especially its habitat, so you learn more about its ecological relationships. Let your curiosity be your guide.

Your notes will be most useful if you have a system for retrieving the information. Computers are ideal for this purpose, and commercial software systems are available for recording, organizing, and retrieving birding observations. Of course, you can also do this with a paper system of your own, or with a system of text files. It depends on what's important to you. Some birders, for instance, want to know migration dates for each species in their area, and they have set up paper or computerized systems to record this information. Others may want to record each time they have seen certain species. And some may simply want to have a set of journals that record pleasant and exciting birding adventures.

A Place to Watch

Although bird watching often starts at home, perhaps by observing a feeder outside your window, it's important to find at least one place for more active birding that meets several criteria:

- It's reasonably quiet. A city park may be good, but not if it's spoiled by traffic noise or if there are a lot of kids running around and making noise, scaring off the birds.
- You can get there easily, so you're inclined to go fairly often. Birding, at least for land birds, is best done early in the morning, and most birders try to be in the field by sunrise.
- You feel safe there, especially early in the morning when there may be few other people around.
- It has enough vegetation to attract a goodly number of birds.
- It has some aquatic habitat — open water (a lake or an ocean view) or a wetland.

The last point isn't essential, but there are advantages to starting your study of birds where you can pay attention to water birds, especially ducks. So a place that attracts migrating or wintering ducks is ideal.

Start Reading

This book is primarily about what to do at home in preparation for going into the field. You can prepare yourself immeasurably just by starting to read about birds and birding. (See the bibliography.) You'll probably want additional books with basic information about North American birds. Books about birding adventures, and more generally about nature study and adventuring, can be an enormous pleasure, and some of the best were written many years ago. You can also gain much by reading books about birds in general and about their behavior, biology, and ecology. As you learn more about birds, it will be easier to identify them, and you will take greater pleasure in watching and studying them. Also, try some of the many books about specific groups of birds and about the birds of certain regions. They generally have gorgeous color plates — a pleasure in themselves — and they can help to put your local observations into perspective.

SOME CAUTIONS

To help you become a better observer and make your experience more joyful, let me warn you about some traps that birders fall into easily.

Rumpelstiltskinism

In the fairy tale "Rumpelstiltskin," a princess who has to weave straw into gold is helped by the strange little man of the title and has power over him only when she can guess his name. My late friend Mark Papworth conceived the idea of

Rumpelstiltskinism: the belief that knowing the name of something gives you power over it, and that you know something important about a thing — a bird, for instance — when you know its name. But all you know is a word. The real importance of knowing a bird's name is that you can start to learn something significant about it — its life, its habits, where it lives, how it lives, and so on. Please don't be satisfied with just knowing its name.

Creative Reconstruction of Memories

We commonly think we observe accurately and that eyewitness accounts of events are dependable. In fact, memory is trickier. Dr. Elizabeth Loftus, of the University of California at Irvine, has made a lifelong study of memory and has been especially interested in eyewitness accounts of crimes. She has demonstrated experimentally just how easily our memories of events — even what we have just observed — can be distorted by casual suggestions. For instance, she has had her class interrupted by an actor rushing in and doing something memorable and outrageous, such as yelling wildly, and then rushing out again. She then has a stooge introduce a suggestion about the intruder; for instance, that he had a mustache. When she brings in a lineup of several possible perpetrators, the students generally single out the one with a mustache. Of course, the actual perpetrator did not have a mustache, and the observers' memories were distorted by the planted suggestion.

This can happen easily during birding. In his helpful book *The Complete Birder,* Jack Connor tells how he was misled while driving along a Florida highway. He spotted what he was sure was a black-and-white hawk, and he convinced himself he had seen a bird with the markings of a Crested Caracara — red on its face and a big hooked bill. With great excitement, he turned around and drove back to the spot. The bird was a piece of plastic flapping in the wind. Connor had creatively reconstructed his observation on the basis of his wishes and his excitement.

I had a similar experience while birding alone in southeastern Arizona, one of the premier birding areas of North America. As I stood on a rise, a falcon flew toward me, and I thought I saw rufous undersides, which made me think of an Aplomado Falcon — a rare possibility in the area. Then I saw in the field guide that the principal field mark of an Aplomado Falcon is a black breast-band. At that moment, I couldn't be sure whether I had seen such a breast-band or not. My mental image of the bird placed a breast-band on it, but I knew enough about observing to realize that I could very well have placed that band on my mental image after looking in the book. Naturally, I didn't count it.

This game we play with ourselves, with our memories and hopes, has been called the *inner game.* This is where ethics and skepticism come into birding.

Birding has a scientific aspect, and the observations of good birders contribute to the science of ornithology. Nonscientists don't realize that science is *a fundamentally moral activity,* based on the moral value of absolute honesty. Scientists have to be truth-tellers, committed to looking at the world objectively, and truthfully reporting their observations or the results of experiments. Poor observers or people who fool themselves distort the process. But science is self-correcting. A scientist who makes erroneous claims, for whatever reason, will be found out when others report that they can't confirm the claims or can't reproduce the reported observations. So scientists — and birders — have to learn to check their enthusiasm, to be particularly skeptical of their observations in proportion to the novelty and importance of what they think they have seen. Because one object of the birding game is to add new birds to our life lists — *lifers* — we have subtle inner motivations to see the critical field marks of a desirable bird, motivations that easily color our observations. One way around the problem is to have two or more independent observers who check each other in the right way. My colleague Steve Herman always tells his students, "Look at the bird, not at the book." One person can focus his binoculars on the bird while someone else looks at the book and asks questions in a checking mode, not in a prompting or suggesting mode. Birders can also preserve objectivity by sketching their observations independently and then comparing notes. This is what Tim Gallagher and Bobby Harrison did in 2004 when they were hoping to find Ivory-billed Woodpeckers surviving in Arkansas; after observing a possible bird, they each made sketches, which turned out to agree with each other and to confirm independent observations of the bird.

Playing this inner game with ourselves is a matter of care and skepticism. If birders aren't honest with themselves and with others, what's the point of playing the game? Only gamblers benefit from cheating at games, and the only gambling I know of in birding is the friendliest wager about some actual or possible observation. Everyone wants to become known as a good player, a trustworthy observer. Someone whose life list becomes suspect or who reports too many rarities unconfirmed by others acquires just the opposite reputation, and then the fun of the game is over.

Impatience

You can probably read this book in a few hours and do all the exercises in it, except for the field exercises, in not much more time. *But it will take you far longer to acquire the skills to which the book tries to guide you.* You know that if you read a book about building up your muscle tone, becoming a skilled woodworker, or learning to play a guitar, it will take you much longer to actually do the activity or acquire the skill than it took to read through the book. This is that kind of book.

This guide outlines strategies to help you advance from the barest acquaintance with birds toward a sort of intermediate level. That journey, however, will take time. Experienced birders urge beginners to learn patience. It may be the most important trait you can acquire; you'll then be able to enjoy your experiences in the field and be happy with your progress. In showing you how to *see* birds, I am introducing a skill that you must practice and develop slowly, over months at least, and probably for the rest of your life. I've been birding seriously since my teens, and I'm still improving my ability to see birds well. I don't expect you to learn the categories of birds immediately, and you'll learn to distinguish the more problematic groups of birds slowly with more field experience and study at home. If you could learn all these things in the time it takes to work through the book once, you would advance from beginner to a skilled intermediate-level birder in just a couple of weeks. That ain't gonna happen.

Beginners often feel discouraged because they see so many birds they can't identify. But this is normal for the game. You will *never* be able to identify every bird you see, and you'll feel better about birding if you know this from the start. In fact, in some places I urge you to ignore whole categories of birds (such as immatures) and not even *try* to learn them. As your skills develop, you'll be able to identify more birds, but even the experts can't identify everything. You'll hear experts discussing puzzling observations, arguing with one another, not sure of just what they have seen.

It is okay to say, "I don't know."

It is okay to say, "That bird might have been either an *X* or a *Y*, and I'm inclined to say *Y* because I saw this feature but not that one, but in the end I can't be sure."

It is okay to question someone else's identification — not only okay, but expected! Birding requires that each person become her own expert and make her own independent observations and judgments. You can even disagree with world-renowned experts — in a tactful, friendly manner, of course — and you have a duty to disagree if you have a good reason for doing so. You may have had a better view or seen the bird in a better light. Settling a disagreement about the identification of a bird is instructive to both parties, because you both have to look at the bird critically and agree on features that are crucial for its identification. Everyone makes mistakes, even experts.

So it is okay to call a bird wrong. We learn by making mistakes. To return to birding and science, in her book *An Imagined World*, the historian of science June Goodfield wrote about how scientists really work by recording the work and thought of a biologist whom she calls Anna. Regarding the spirit of science, Anna says, "Above all, there is freedom, the knowledge that you are going to make mistakes and not being afraid. . . . By the end of that time I was dropping mistakes right, left, and center. I learned to love making mistakes." And again, later: "In science . . . it is very important that you do make mistakes and, even more, that you are not ashamed or worried about them. Only then can you progress." So make your mistakes as fast as you can.

Your Personal Interests and Abilities

I'm afraid birders sometimes get the impression that if they don't reach the level of the experts who seemingly can instantly identify every North American bird, they have failed in some way. But whether you enjoy birding or butterflying or identifying plants, you should feel free to do it as much or as little as you please, to reach your own level of expertise — without apologizing.

People differ in the acuteness of their senses. After all, very few of us become star tennis or baseball players, prima ballerinas, or concert pianists. Those who excel at such activities must be blessed with certain skills. I've been with birders whose eyes, I'm convinced, are simply more acute than others' at seeing fine details; certainly, just about everyone's ears are better than mine. But we can all take the same pleasure in the joy of the experience and our ability to identify what we see and hear.

CHAPTER 2

Learning How to See

I am standing in a beautiful garden at the Summer Palace in Lhasa, Tibet. I have never been to this part of the world before. Just a few minutes before, I enjoyed the spectacular sight of large green Derbyan Parakeets perched in the tops of pine trees, feeding on the cones. I have no idea what might appear next. Noticing some movement in the bare branches of a tree nearby, I start to bring my binoculars up to focus on it. A part of my mind has already eliminated several categories of birds that couldn't possibly be there and is open to the most likely categories that I might see. As soon as I've seen one small bird clearly, my mind immediately clicks to *small warbler,* and I know I'm observing some very small birds with a warbler form — thin, insect-eating, warbler bills and some yellow coloration. I immediately start to look for specific features and make a mental list:

> Yellowish wash on breast
> Black eye line
> Clear white supercilium
> Light grayish back
> No wing bars

Feeling that I've seen enough to consult the book, a field guide to the birds of China, I find the plates with small warblers of this kind and almost immediately locate what I've seen: Tickell's Leaf Warbler. I'm confident of my identification, and the map in the book confirms that the bird should be found in this region.

SEEING

I tell this story to illustrate the difference between *naive looking* and *seeing as a birder sees.* It raises the whole question of what seeing is all about, since birding is primarily about seeing — and hearing, too, but what I say about seeing will carry over to hearing. A simple view of seeing is that light comes into our eyes and forms a picture on the retinas, and then that picture somehow goes into the brain, and we see, directly and naively. But this simple conception is clearly wrong. The philosopher of science N. R. Hanson developed a more realistic view of seeing, especially in his book *Perception and Discovery*. Hanson argued convincingly that seeing and knowing are intimately connected and that what we perceive depends on what we know — is shaped by what we know. We perceive the world, Hanson contended, through theories about the world; he referred to these theories as "spectacles behind the eyeballs" and demonstrated his ideas in part by means of ambiguous figures, such as this well-known figure, called a Necker cube:

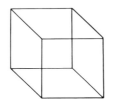

Look at the cube: Are you seeing it from above, looking down on the top; or from below, looking up at the bottom? Whichever way you started to see it, now try to change your perspective and see it the other way. Once you have done this, notice that by a subtle change in viewpoint you can decide to see it one way or the other. In other words, your perception of the cube depends on which *internal hypothesis* you are entertaining at the moment, and you can choose to switch hypotheses. Similarly, look at this:

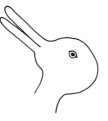

You could see this figure as either a duck or a rabbit, and again you can change hypotheses in midlook, choosing to see it one way or the other. But you cannot choose to see the Necker cube or the duck-rabbit figure as just a bunch of lines. You always see it *as* something, and this is the first point of the argument: We do not see the world naively, we *see as*.

Yet we can be mistaken in seeing. Driving along a highway one day (birding, of course), I approached a pickup truck. As I came closer, I saw a rather oddly shaped white thing on the back of the truck that looked like a sheepskin draped over the tailgate. Suddenly, as I got nearer, my perception changed. What I had perceived as the top edge of the tailgate became the front of the truck bed, and the oddly shaped object became a white dog standing in the bed. And the change in perception was just as sudden as the change you experience in seeing the cube from above or below, or in seeing the other figure as a duck or as a rabbit.

Moreover, Hanson argued, we do not merely *see as;* we also *see that.* Once we see an object *as* something, everything we know about the object comes into play and we perceive those characteristics. For instance, if you see the Necker cube from above, you also see that the top is a surface that could support something, depending on whether you imagine it to be made of wire, plastic, or something more substantial. Now consider seeing this:

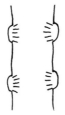

It doesn't take much imagination to see this as a bear climbing a tree as seen from the other side of the tree. That means you also see that if you were to walk around, you would see this:

That knowledge of what you would see enters into the seeing, becomes a part of it.

With this background, it's easy to understand how we can fool ourselves in birding, as I discussed in chapter 1. Since we see the world through our hypotheses, expectations, and knowledge, we hypothesize that the bird before us is an exceedingly exciting rare bird that we have been trying to add to our life list for at least ten years. Here it is! Wow! It has all the critical field marks . . . doesn't it? Or does it? Here is where enthusiasm and wishful thinking can turn one species into another. 'Nuff said.

Birding is a matter of seeing and hearing accurately, and it begins with the simple experience of looking at a bird. But notice that I didn't say "seeing a bird." I believe the critical experience that separates a birder from a nonbirder occurs right there, at the junction between *looking at* the bird and *seeing it in the right way.* This is the crucial point that defines what you must be aiming for, and I believe it is twofold. Part of your goal is to become so familiar with many species that you perceive each bird *as the particular bird that it is* — that you don't just see it naively as a mass of feathers of a certain color but that you perceive it *as* a Song Sparrow or *as* a Rusty Blackbird or *as* a Swainson's Thrush. But you will never become familiar with every kind of bird in the world, and even some common birds will present unusual challenges, such as distinctive immature plumages or unusual appearances connected with molting. Thus, the second and more important goal is being able to see the world in the way I was able to see the Tickell's Leaf Warblers for the first time. That means learning to *see that* certain things are true of the bird. For instance:

- *That* its bill is a conical bill shaped for eating seeds; or a very thin bill shaped for catching small insects; or a rather long curved bill shaped for eating insects, fruit, or worms; or a hooked bill shaped for tearing flesh; or . . .
- *That* its overall form is thin and elongated; or fat and chubby; or compact and almost tailless; or . . .
- *That* its tail is short and held erect; or long and held downward; or rounded at the end; or notched at the end; or that it has a distinctive white patch; or . . .
- *That* its wings are short and round; or long and pointed; or . . .
- *That* it has a distinct ring around its eyes; or a distinct color stripe over the eye; or a distinct colored line going through the eye; or a black line descending from the bill; or . . .
- *That* it flicks its wings repeatedly; or keeps slowly lowering its tail; or hangs upside down in the branches; or . . .
- *That* there are two distinct bars on its wing; or one light bar; or a white patch on the wing; or no bars at all; or . . .

And so on. This *collection of specific points to see* will constitute your personal spectacles behind your eyeballs. These are the characteristics — the field marks — you will use for identifying each kind of bird. This habit of perceiving particular features of the bill, the wings, the tail, and so on, as well as behavioral details, will be essential throughout your lifetime of observing birds as you see new kinds of birds and as you run up against challenges, birds that you can't easily identify and must puzzle out on the basis of the particular features you have learned to observe so carefully.

All this goes for hearing, too. Experienced birders know they will hear far more birds than they can see, at least in habitats such as woodlands, and they become familiar with birds' voices so they can walk through a woodland thinking, *There are Brown Creepers over there, and Golden-crowned Kinglets up in the treetops; I hear Song Sparrows over here, and that's a Willow Flycatcher just to my right.* These perceptions of hearing depend on paying attention to particular features of the voice, analogous to observing particular features of the bird's anatomy or plumage.

STARTING TO SEE BIRDS

For some initial lessons in seeing, let's focus here on three characteristics: types of bills, general body shape and posture, and features of tails.

Bills

We'll begin by looking at the bills of selected birds of quite different types, noting what each bird eats.

Heron
eats fish, frogs,
various small animals

Pelican
scoops up large
numbers of fish

Duck
eats mostly water plants

Hawk
eats various
small animals

Shorebird
picks tiny animals out
of the sand and mud

Parrot
eats mostly fruits
and seeds

Hummingbird
probes into flowers to extract
nectar and some insects

Nighthawk
scoops insects out
of the air while flying

Woodpecker
digs into trees
to extract insects

Of course the nearly 10,000 species of birds on earth have many ways of getting food, with appropriately specialized bills. The first take-home lesson is the importance of *noticing a bird's bill* and thinking of it as the bird's primary — only, in most cases — tool for getting food. We mammals need to be reminded of this, especially because we humans are so used to manipulating tools and holding food with our skilled prehensile hands. Birds are different. Most avian predators, especially hawks and owls, use their feet for grasping their food, and some sparrows use their feet for digging in the leaf litter to uncover food, but all birds depend on their bills to get food, and the shape of the bill naturally reflects its use.

EXERCISE 2-1. Now let's focus on some of the songbirds, the largest major category of birds. We'll look at the bills of some birds and consider them in relationship to the birds' foods. As we do this, keep in mind the general principle of zoology that the size of an animal's mouth is proportional to the size of its food: Big mouths eat big things, small mouths eat small things.

Let's start with three types of birds that eat mostly insects:

Wren   **Kinglet**   **Warbler**

These are small birds, and their bills are very small and thin. Now compare them with some birds that supplement their insect diets with other food:

Vireo   **Blackbird**   **Meadowlark**
mostly insects,   insects and seeds   insects and seeds
some berries

Notice that vireos, birds that are similar in size to warblers, have slightly larger, heavier bills than the strict insect eaters, such as warblers and kinglets. This fits with their more varied diets. And look at the blackbirds and meadowlarks, birds that add seeds to their diet of insects. Compare their bills to those of some birds that are more specialized for eating seeds:

Goldfinch   **Sparrow**   **Grosbeak**
mostly seeds, some insects   mostly seeds and insects   insects, seeds, some berries

Finally, consider some birds with different and more varied diets:

Robin
insects, earthworms, other
invertebrates; berries

Blue Jay
omnivorous
(eats everything)

Shrike
small birds, large insects,
rodents

Using this brief survey, make some notes about some of the types of bills found among songbirds and what shapes of bills correlate with different foods.

_____

_____

_____

_____

_____

_____

_____

_____

_____

Sparrows and finches have bills with the strength to crush seeds; the bills are usually described as *conical*, but since we don't generally get three-dimensional views of them, they might better be described as *triangular, deep,* or *heavy.* It is well known from studies of certain species — such as the finches of the Galápagos Islands — that the typical bill size of each species is closely correlated with the size of the seeds it eats. Insect eaters, in contrast to seed eaters, have smaller bills that are adapted for eating softer foods, and some species have rather elongated, sometimes curved bills that they use for ferreting insects out of holes, cracks, or the depths of flowers.

The size and shape of a bird's bill is one of the first things you should learn to see. Since House Sparrows are easy to find, go out and observe them from a distance of about 10 to 20 feet, with and without binoculars. Their bills are small, but you can train yourself to see the conical (triangular) shape both in good light and silhouetted against a light background. If you can find some of the other species shown here, study them, too, paying particular attention to their bills. Also, think about how their bills are used. You can observe this for yourself by watching some of these birds forage for a while.

Overall Shape and Posture

Here are two groups of common birds. Look at them critically and try to see what the members of one group have in common that sets them off from the other group.

Group 1

Blue Jay

Brown Thrasher

Gray Catbird

Blue-gray Gnatcatcher

Group 2

American Robin

Western Meadowlark

European Starling

Ruby-crowned Kinglet

These birds differ in shape, either long and slim (group 1) or more compact (group 2). The difference lies in a combination of the body itself, the tail, and maybe the bill. Gnatcatchers and kinglets are both small; their bodies are similar, but a gnatcatcher's long tail makes it a slim, elongated bird, whereas a kinglet is chunky. As you gain more experience in watching birds and are able to watch both gnatcatchers and kinglets forage in trees, you'll see how the gnatcatcher's elongated form contrasts with that of a kinglet or warbler. Robins and Blue Jays both are common around residential areas in the East, but look at the difference in their overall shapes, ignoring the obvious differences in their plumages.

The point may become even clearer in silhouettes:

Even in poor light, when a bird is just a dark silhouette against the sky, you can get a good impression of its general form that will narrow down its identity.

In addition, look at the birds' postures. Some of them stand quite erect, with their heads up and their tails down. Others tend to assume more horizontal positions, maybe with their tails up in the air, and you may already have noticed some little birds such as chickadees and kinglets hanging upside down in trees. Seeing birds also means noticing how they stand and move.

Jizz

As we begin to distinguish birds on the basis of their overall shape and behavior, we are starting to talk about what birders call a bird's *jizz:* a subtle, characteristic combination of its size and shape, its posture, and its ways of moving. A bird's jizz is the *impression* it gives you, often so subtle that you can't describe it to others but also so definite that you know the bird, even at a distance. (In *The Ardent Birder,* Todd Newberry likens it to recognizing a friend at a distance, so even before you can see a face, subtle clues tell you it's Beth rather than Ellen or Maggie.) A birder urban legend is that this term originated in the Royal Air Force during World War II, when the aviators learned the *giss* of each type of airplane, a word that stood for "general impression of size and shape." While relevant to airplane identification, the term *jizz* was first brought into the birding vocabulary in 1922 by the British ornithologist T. A. Coward (1877–1933). Coward said he had learned the word from a west coast Irishman who knew the local species of wildlife by their jizz, meaning subtle and almost indescribable features of form and behavior. As you advance in birding, you'll become familiar with the jizz of more and more species, so you'll be able to call them correctly as soon as you see them.

FIELD EXERCISE

Using the range maps in your field guide, try to locate some of the common birds pictured above. Watch them carefully, and as they move, compare them to their silhouettes. Ignore their colors. Pay particular attention to each bird's overall form. Try to connect the silhouette to the living bird and start to develop a feeling for the jizz of each species. Convince yourself that you can recognize the bird from just its general shape and posture in combination with its ways of moving.

Tails

Tails often carry valuable field marks in their shapes, colors, and patterns. It is often critical to note whether the end of a tail is flat or straight (2), notched (3), or rounded (4). Some tails are deeply forked (1) or pointed (5). Furthermore,

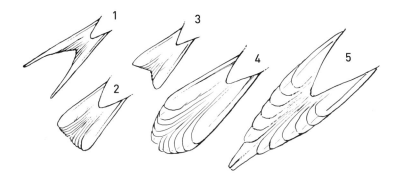

tails may have distinctive plumages, such as white outer feathers in contrast to central feathers of another color. It is not uncommon to see an obscurely

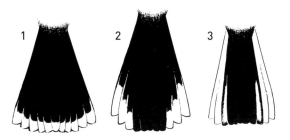

plumaged bird with its tail hidden and no other obvious marks to identify it that suddenly turns its back toward you or flies away and reveals in its tail the critical field marks that identify it. Or some feature of the tail may let you exclude one group of species or another, narrowing your choices. To see this, try these challenges, which focus on tails. (Remember, E = Peterson's eastern guide, W = his western guide.)

EXERCISE 2-2. E313, 315; W309, 311. Describe the difference between the tails of a Red-winged Blackbird and a Brown-headed Cowbird.

_____

_____

EXERCISE 2-3. How do the tails of small finches such as the American Goldfinch and Pine Siskin (E291; W345) differ from those of some common sparrows (E301; W325)?

_____

_____

EXERCISE 2-4. E311; W307. How do the tails of common blackbirds (Brewer's, Rusty) differ from those of the various grackles?

_____

_____

EXERCISE 2-5. E313, 315, 319; W309, 311, 347. If a brownish bird in a grassland has its back to you, how can you distinguish a female or winter Bobolink from a meadowlark or Dickcissel?

_____

_____

_____

EXERCISE 2-6. What overall difference can you see between the tails of gulls and terns in flight (E173–89; W89–109)?

_____

_____

EXERCISE 2-7. E201; W213. From just the markings on their tails, how do you tell a Black-billed Cuckoo from a Yellow-billed Cuckoo?

_____

_____

EXERCISE 2-8. E253; W253. How can the shape of the tail help you distinguish a crow from a raven in flight?

_____

_____

EXERCISE 2-9. In a grassland, a large bird springs up in front of you and flies away — maybe a grouse or a prairie chicken (E123; W161). What can you see as it flies away that will help you distinguish one from the other?

_____

_____

_____

EXERCISE 2-10. E283, 317; W313, 315. Orioles and tanagers are similar in that the males are brightly colored — yellow, orange, and red — and the females are yellow or yellow-green. Find three general features that distinguish one group from the other. This question is not limited to features of the tail, so you'll have to look at all aspects of these birds. Write a few words about these features in each group.

_____

_____

_____

_____

DRAWING HELPS A LOT

A classic story of science involves a student who came to study under Professor Louis Agassiz, one of the giants of 19th-century natural history. Agassiz assigned him to study a preserved fish, but gave no other instructions. After a while, the student decided to draw the fish. Agassiz approved, saying, "That is right. A pencil is one of the best eyes." It is indeed. Drawing forces the eye to see details, even if the hand is unskilled. Drawing the birds you see in the field right in your notebook is especially valuable in learning to see birds' features and to identify them. You don't have to be a fine artist to do so. (If you want to become really excellent at drawing, use Betty Edwards's book *Drawing on the Right Side of the Brain*.) But anyone can draw a bird easily by using a simple method. It begins, appropriately, with an egg.

You can make the egg relatively fat and compact or relatively narrow and extended to fit the body of the bird you're observing. Then add a head.

As you add the head, you can pay attention to the size and shape of the bill and to details such as the crown being relatively flat (low in profile) or rounded (high in profile), or whether the bird has a crest.

Then add a tail. Here you can pay attention to its length, to add to the impression of a compact bird or an elongated bird.

Add a wing, noting where the wingtip falls relative to the end of the tail.

Then you can add other features of plumage, such as wing bars, as discussed in chapter 5. In only a minute or two, you can make a perfectly acceptable and very useful sketch like this in your field notes. You'll find these sketches valuable as learning tools, and by annotating them with comments, you will make them by far the best way of recording the features of birds that are hard to identify in the field.

BIRDERS' COLORS

Birders rather casually use terms for colors that many other people don't know, even those who are familiar with the colors of clothing or decorative schemes for homes. Here are the most common of these terms.

Buff or buffy: a moderate orange-yellow
Cinnamon: yellowish tan
Chestnut: similar to rufous, but closer to brown
Ocher: an earthy yellowish color
Olive: yellowish green, but not strongly saturated
Rufous: reddish brown
Slate or slaty: dark gray

CHAPTER 3

Learning Categories

"Hey, I saw this bird the other day, and it had a lot of red on its head and a long tail and it was pecking away at something on the ground. What do you think it could have been?" Nonbirdy friends often ask me questions like that. I immediately ask, "What *general kind* of a bird was it? Was it a little songbird or a shorebird or a hawk or a wading bird or a woodpecker or a chickenlike bird or what?" But they usually don't know. If pressed, most people recognize that there are different general kinds of birds. They know the difference between some nebulous group that includes sparrows and canaries and another nebulous group that includes chickens and turkeys, but they don't think about those categories. In becoming a birder, however, you have to start thinking this way and start learning categories of birds.

MAKING SENSE OF THE FIELD GUIDE

After thumbing through a field guide or trying desperately to find a picture of a bird he or she has seen, a beginner often wants to scream in frustration, "Why is the field guide organized in such a crazy way? Why don't they just list birds alphabetically or put the birds together by color, or maybe size, or maybe by the places they live?" To help you understand why the checklists and field guides are organized as they are, I'll explain the formal categories of birds, the ones ornithologists use. Birders learn them, and you, too, can gradually add the names of these categories to your vocabulary.

One foundation of biology is the science of taxonomy, or systematics, which is all about classifying organisms on the basis of their similarities and differences. The modern way of classification was devised in the mid-18th century by Carl von Linné, best known by his Latinized name, Carolus Linnaeus. Linnaeus started to classify species with a *hierarchy*, a system of categories that include smaller categories that include still smaller categories. The biological hierarchy begins with *kingdoms* — such as bacteria, plants, animals, and fungi — which include *phyla* (singular *phylum*); a phylum is divided into *classes*, the classes into *orders,* and thence down the line to *families, genera* (singular *genus*), and *species.* Since these categories (called *taxa;* the singular is *taxon*) are usually not enough to express all the desired detail, systematists sometimes expand the hierarchy by using the prefixes *super-, sub-,* and *infra-,* and by interpolating other categories. Thus, a suborder may be divided into superfamilies, then families, subfamilies, and tribes, each including one or more genera. For example, the common Rose-breasted Grosbeak, *Pheucticus ludovicianus,* fits into one modern classification like this:

> Class Aves
> > Subclass Neornithes
> > > Order Passeriformes
> > > > Family Fringillidae
> > > > > Subfamily Emberizinae
> > > > > > Tribe Cardinalini
> > > > > > > Genus *Pheucticus*

All the organisms in a taxon share certain features. In the animal kingdom, for instance, the phylum Chordata includes all the animals that have a rod of cartilage, called a notochord, down the middle of the back. All of us critters that have the notochord replaced by backbones, or vertebrae — fish, amphibians, reptiles, birds, and mammals — belong to the subphylum Vertebrata. This is the subphylum that interests us here, as it includes the class Aves, the birds. Aves is divided into many orders, whose names end in *-formes,* pronounced *form-ease.* All orders include at least one family (whose names end in *-idae,* pronounced *ih-dee*), and some families are divided into subfamilies (whose names all end in *-inae*). The life lists in the Peterson Field Guides (E14–23; W409–15) provide this whole classification for the birds of North America in a sequence established by the American Ornithologists' Union (AOU), the authority for this information in our region. The sequence of orders reflects the current scientific view of how the principal types of birds evolved, with the most primitive orders first. Worldwide checklists begin with some orders that don't concern us in North America, including such beasts as ostriches and emus. For a long time, the AOU list started with the loons and grebes and ended with the large order Passeriformes, the familiar singing and perching birds, commonly called passerines. However, the checklist sequence has recently been revised somewhat, on the basis of new DNA evidence about relationships among the birds, placing ducks and gallinaceous (chickenlike) birds first.

So the answer to the question "Why are the field guides organized in such a crazy way?" is "We are looking at living organisms that are related to one another to various degrees, as reflected by a classification." Checklists then present species in the sequences of the classification, and the books are generally organized in the same way. You can be a fine birder without knowing the whole classification of birds, but you'll have a more thorough sense of the staggering variety of birds if you do learn it and use it to sort out the similarities and differences that suggest their evolutionary relationships.

The Peterson Field Guides essentially follow the standard checklist sequence — see the table of contents in each — and Peterson uses some large informal groupings, such as "ducks and ducklike swimming birds." Peterson gives the names of orders in the life lists but otherwise uses only family names — for example, the family Anseridae instead of the order Anseriformes.

DRAWING MAJOR TYPES OF BIRDS

Before looking at the 21 orders into which North American birds are classified, try this drawing exercise to help you start recognizing the principal characteristics of these birds. Go through the field guide, looking carefully at the birds in the groups named below, and make a simple sketch to represent each, seeking to create a kind of *average* representation that captures the *gestalt* of the group. The German word *gestalt* means "general form." The gestalt should reflect the *overall body form* and the size and shape of the bill, which may be harder to see immediately. This exercise extends the lessons of chapter 2 by focusing on these features, and the objective is to help you mature in birding sophistication by developing a personal collection of gestalts (okay, *gestalten*, if you want to stick with the German) that fit the major categories of birds. *Gestalt* is obviously closely connected to *jizz*, and I wouldn't want anyone to press me too closely on the distinction, but *gestalt* pertains to form and is characteristic of a group of birds, whereas *jizz* also includes subtle factors of a bird's movement and behavior and refers to individual species. In any case, you may be zipping along a highway at 60 miles per hour and catch a glimpse of a tall bird wading at the edge of a pond; that brief glimpse should immediately call up your heron-or-egret gestalt, so you know right away what general type of bird it is — a tall wader — even if you can't tell whether you just saw a heron, egret, ibis, or even a stork.

This drawing exercise should not only extend the lesson from chapter 2 about drawing birds in a simple way but should also show the importance of looking at silhouettes, as shown on the endpapers of your field guides. Peterson emphasized that many common birds have such unique shapes that we can recognize them just by their silhouettes, even in terrible light or with only a glimpse of their form. And a silhouette not only captures the forms of the few common birds shown on the endpapers but also captures the gestalts of the various orders and other large taxa. So I believe your drawings will be most useful if they are just outlines, which you could fill in to create a silhouette. For example, consider a group that isn't included below, the rails (E129, 131; W119). These are little chickenlike marsh birds, generally secretive and hard to see. They all have the same kind of bent-over posture, with short, erect tails; necks of short to moderate length; long toes; and heavy bills, sometimes quite long. An average rail silhouette might be:

Now with this example in mind, consult your field guide pictures and make your sketches, aiming for a drawing of an "average" bird of each type.

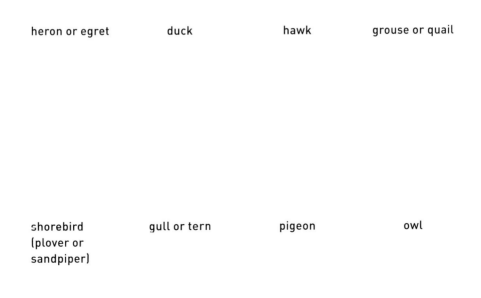

| heron or egret | duck | hawk | grouse or quail |

| shorebird (plover or sandpiper) | gull or tern | pigeon | owl |

hummingbird   woodpecker   passerine
                                                             (robin or sparrow, for instance)

When you are finished with your drawings, consider the following questions.

EXERCISE 3-1. Think about how the *body* of each type of bird is oriented, even though its neck may stick up in the air. Which groups have essentially *vertical* bodies and which essentially *horizontal*?

_____

_____

_____

_____

_____

_____

EXERCISE 3-2. List some groups of birds that are large and some that are small.

_____

_____

_____

_____

In light of our previous emphasis on the bill as a bird's primary tool for getting food, go back to your sketches and the paintings of these birds in your field guide and think about their bills. Will you recognize birds of some categories largely on this basis? Read the paragraph introducing each major group of birds, where Peterson has brief notes about their food, and try to relate the shapes of the birds' bills to their food.

EXERCISE 3-3. What does the sharply curved bill of a hawk or owl tell you, in comparison to the long spearlike bill of a heron or egret?

_____

_____

EXERCISE 3-4. Considering that grouse and quail are in the same category as chickens, and that you know generally what chickens eat, what do you think the bills of these birds are good for?

_____

_____

EXERCISE 3-5. Where are you most likely to see a gull or tern, and on what will it be feeding?

_____

_____

_____

A QUICK ROMP THROUGH THE ORDERS

Leaving ducks and some other water birds for a later section, follow along in the field guide as we survey the other orders to help you develop your feeling for the great variety of bird types.

GALLIFORMES: QUAIL, GROUSE, PTARMIGAN, AND TURKEYS. Although they are located in the middle of the field guides (E120–25; W158–67), the gallinaceous birds have been moved closer to the front of the AOU checklist. Look at their small bills and rounded wings and at their generally streaked brown color, which camouflages them so well in the grasslands they commonly inhabit. They ought to be familiar, even to urban people, who generally see their chickens and turkeys wrapped in plastic in the supermarket. The galliforms are all variations on chickens; our common chickens were derived from the Red Jungle fowl of east Asia.

PROCELLARIIFORMES: ALBATROSSES, SHEARWATERS, PETRELS.

These are oceanic birds, called tubenoses because of their peculiar bill structure (E30). We see them mostly on pelagic (oceanic) birding trips several miles off-shore, where they feed on fish, squid, crustaceans, and carrion. Sometimes, however, they come close to the land, and a flock of thousands might appear over a bay off the ocean. Note their typically dark upper surfaces with white undersides and wing linings.

PELECANIFORMES: PELICANS AND CORMORANTS.

The pelican, as Dixon Merritt observed in a limerick, is a wonderful bird whose "bill will hold more than his belican." With their huge long bills and throat pouches, they are hard to mistake for anything else (E39; W85). Cormorants are large black snaky-necked birds, easily distinguished from ducks and other water birds. The order also includes some other sea birds: gannets, boobies, and tropicbirds.

CICONIIFORMES: HERONS, EGRETS, IBISES, STORKS.

These birds, usu-ally called waders, haunt our marshes and shorelines. (A potential confusion is that Europeans call shorebirds waders.) A silhouette representing the most typi-cal birds on E46–59 or W110–17 must show a tall bird with a long neck often bent into an S-shape, with either a heavy spearlike bill (herons and egrets) or a heavy downcurved bill (ibises). Some species (bitterns, night-herons: E51; W115) are much smaller, with little or no neck. The delicate plumes of egrets were once prized by milliners, and plume hunters almost drove these birds to ex-tinction; saving them was the founding battle of the Audubon Society. Waders include spoonbills and flamingos, with their lovely plumage and very odd bills, although flamingos are assigned to an order of their own, Phoenicopteriformes; Greater Flamingos are often seen at Everglades National Park in Florida.

FALCONIFORMES: OSPREY, EAGLES, HAWKS, FALCONS.

These are so familiar in a general way that they hardly require any comment now, but they present enough identification problems to beginners to warrant a separate chap-ter for analysis (chapter 13).

GRUIFORMES: RAILS, CRANES, COOTS. I used rails above as an example. We'll look at coots later in comparison to other water birds. Cranes look like herons (E57; W117), but they fly with their necks extended, whereas herons and egrets fly with their necks folded back. We have only two cranes in North America; to see Whooping Cranes, you just about have to go to the Aransas National Wildlife Refuge in Texas, although the birds do migrate over the Midwest. Sandhill Cranes are more widespread.

CHARADRIIFORMES (SHOREBIRDS): PLOVERS, SANDPIPERS. Although this group (E132–67; W120–57) includes some tall birds, most shorebirds are squat and horizontal-bodied with erect heads and thin bills, sometimes very long bills. They feed on mud flats and beaches, but also on grasslands and rocky coasts, ferreting out insects and other small animals. Peterson notes that beginners find them confusing, so chapter 14 is devoted to analyzing them.

CHARADRIIFORMES: GULLS AND TERNS. Gulls are so common that everyone knows their general appearance. Sorting them out is challenging, however, so they are addressed in chapter 15. Terns are more delicate, more graceful and fairylike.

CHARADRIIFORMES: ALCIDS. The Antarctic has its black-and-white penguins, the Arctic its black-and-white alcids (family Alcidae: E192–95; W32–37). These are oceanic birds, seen most often in their great colonies nesting on the rocky faces of the north Atlantic and north Pacific coasts.

COLUMBIFORMES: PIGEONS, DOVES. Who doth not know a dove? (There is no formal difference between pigeons and doves, although *dove* is more often applied to the smaller birds.) The common domestic pigeon — Rock Pigeon, formerly named Rock Dove — is sometimes a little too familiar. Notice that they are quite small-headed birds. Most of our pigeons and doves have somber plumages, but a browse through a monograph about the family as a whole will show you how brilliantly colored some of them can be.

PSITTACIFORMES: PARROTS AND PARAKEETS. Everyone interested in birds can recognize these birds easily (see E199; W211). North America's only common parrot, the Carolina Parakeet, became extinct early in the last century. Today's native wild populations of parrots are confined to Texas, from Mexican birds moving over the border. But many urban colonies have been established across the country by escapees, especially Monk Parakeets. Few of the other colonies of escaped birds survive long.

CUCULIFORMES: CUCKOOS, ANIS, AND ROADRUNNERS. (See E201; W213.) Although roadrunners don't call *beep! beep!* and move their legs like wheels, they are unmistakable. The cuckoos are slender, long-tailed, long-billed birds, and though we don't see them often, they are surprisingly common in the eastern and central parts of the continent. Knowledgeable birders find them through their loud, distinctive voices and recognize them by their shape and their characteristic flight pattern. We have two species of ani (AH-nee), long and slender like cuckoos, but all black and with huge bills.

STRIGIFORMES: OWLS. Another unmistakable group, constituting a distinct order, different from falconiforms. Although many owls do hunt by day, most owls are nighttime predators, leaving the hawks and falcons to occupy the niche of daytime predators. Some owls have distinct, erect "ears" and others do not; some owls are very small, hardly bigger than many of the songbirds they hunt.

CAPRIMULGIFORMES: NIGHTHAWKS AND OTHER NIGHTJARS. Also called goatsuckers (E209–11; W215); apparently some people really did believe they suck the milk of goats. The overall gestalt of a sitting nightjar is unique and distinctive. So is the brown dead-leaf feather pattern. They commonly sit on the leafy ground or perch on a heavy tree branch, parallel to the branch, and they can be mistaken for just another part of the  tree. These are mostly birds of the dusk and nighttime, although we sometimes see nighthawks by day. We hear their weird, jarring calls in the night, and to find them we have to go into the night with strong flashlights, perhaps playing recordings of their voices.

TROGONIFORMES: TROGONS. These are gorgeous rarities of areas just north of the Mexican border (W207), and you'll have no doubt about the identity of a trogon as you stand fixed in place, struck by the beauty of such a bird.

APODIFORMES: HUMMINGBIRDS, SWIFTS. How strange it must seem to place the gorgeous tiny hummingbirds (Trochilidae: E213; W216–21) in the same order as the swifts (Apodidae: E234; W247), which resemble swallows and are often confused with them. But *a-pod-* means "without feet," and while it isn't literally true for either group, they both have very small feet and are primarily fliers. Because hummingbirds are so easily attracted to many garden flowers and to feeders, they are familiar to gardeners and people who have learned about common birds by feeding them. All hummers — no, they don't know the words — present the same gestalt of a tiny, brilliant hovering imp of a bird with a long thin bill. Swifts, on the other hand, are generally gray and white in color and are remarkable fliers. A small swift looks like a cigar with wings, as Peterson says, and it flaps its wings . . . swiftly. It takes some fieldwork to learn to see them as different from swallows.

CORACIIFORMES: KINGFISHERS. These distinctive little fishers perch over lakes and streams and then dive in to catch fish very efficiently. Over most of North America, the Belted Kingfisher is the only one you'll see (E215; W207). You must venture to southern Texas to meet the others.

PICIFORMES: WOODPECKERS. Here is a group whose gestalt we recognize almost immediately: an erect bird clinging to a tree or a branch and pecking away at it. And an order distinct from the passerines, or perching birds; most woodpeckers are adapted for clinging to trees with zygodactyl feet — two toes in front and two behind — in contrast to the perching bird's pattern of three toes in front and one behind (anisodactyl).

PASSERIFORMES: PERCHING BIRDS, SONGBIRDS. These are the familiar birds, such as thrushes, flycatchers, warblers, and sparrows, which we will discuss in more detail later.

DUCKS AND OTHER WATER BIRDS

FIELD EXERCISE. This exercise is best done where a lot of water birds winter or can be seen in migration simply to go look at ducks and other water birds, and identify as many as possible. Before going into the field, study your field guide and the following analyses through p. 40. Aside from the fun of birding on a winter day, focusing on water birds presents the opportunity to establish the idea of categories of birds more firmly when you distinguish ducks from other water birds and identify the three main categories of ducks (outlined below).

In looking at ducks, the objective is to categorize them into three groups, which we can do by looking at their typical plumages, the way they feed, and how they take flight or fly.

DUCK GROUPS

	Dabbling (Marsh) Ducks	Diving (Bay and Sea) Ducks	Mergansers
Plumage	Males have bright plumages; females dappled brown	Mostly black, gray, and white plumages	Males sharply black (green-black) and white; females rusty and gray
Feeding	Feed on vegetation in fields or on water by "dabbling," tipping up their tails and extending their necks downward	Feed on plants, shellfish, crayfish, or fish by diving; almost never found on land	Feed on fish by diving
Flight	Fly by springing directly up from the water	Fly by skittering over the water, gradually rising like an airplane	Fly "like an arrow," with bodies horizontal and neck, body, and tail in a straight line

Most male dabbling ducks are easily identified by their bright colors (the females are generally nondescript mottled brown). Though some male diving ducks have subtle green or purple glosses in their black plumage, and male Common and Red-breasted Mergansers have greenish heads, these colors are visible only in favorable light, and from a distance they generally just look black. I think it is always a pleasure to see mergansers. The white of the Common Merganser verges on ivory; the male Hooded Merganser is a majestic fellow; and female mergansers have lovely rusty brown heads with distinctive crests.

When you go out and observe, these are some points about the species that you'll probably see:

1. THE DABBLERS (These notes are primarily about the male birds.)

- **Mallard:** enjoy the green head and chestnut breast of the male in bright sunlight; violet-blue speculum — a *speculum* is a colored patch on the back edge of the wing.

- **American Black Duck**: very dark brown, light brown head, dark purple speculum.

- **Gadwall**: gray body, black rump, light brown head.

- **Northern Shoveler**: rusty flanks and a large spoon-shaped bill.

- **Northern Pintail**: white neck stripe, distinctive long pintail.

- **American Wigeon**: white forehead and cap with green sides to the head.

- **Green-winged Teal**: small size, rich chestnut-and-green head pattern, white vertical slash on the forward flanks, conspicuous yellow patch at the rump, green speculum.

- **Blue-winged Teal**: white crescent moon on the male's face; both sexes have light blue patches on their wings.

- **Wood Duck**: splendidly aberrant, its brilliant colors make it unmistakable.

2. THE DIVERS

- **Bufflehead**: the smallest North American duck. Male has a conspicuous white head patch. The male is so white overall that from a distance you will see a white object on the water, almost a sure sign of a Bufflehead. (But male Common Mergansers and gulls also appear all white.) White patch on the female's cheek. Also flies with an exceptionally fast wingbeat.

- **Goldeneyes**: striking yellow eyes, set in head of an unusual, rather triangular shape, with obvious white patches on the male's face: either a spot (Common) or a comma (Barrow's). The forehead of Barrow's is very steep, that of Common less so, but still distinctive compared with other diving ducks.

- **Scaups**: easily recognized male pattern of black at the head and tail, with white and gray between. Close observation shows that Lesser Scaup has a sloping forehead and a peaked crown whereas Greater Scaup has a steeper forehead and a rounded crown. On the females, the white area surrounding the bill is distinctive.

- **Ring-necked Duck**: like a black-backed scaup, with a vertical white patch just behind the black breast. Both sexes have a gray bill with a white band.

- **Canvasback**: a long, heavy, sloping head and bill. In good light, male's head is chestnut.

- **Redhead**: male has the typical diving-duck pattern of black and white, but the head is chestnut. Gray bill with a white band and black tip.

- **Harlequin Duck**: slaty gray color with patches of white make the male unmistakable.

- **Scoters**: males are almost all black; females are dark brown. Seen more often on salt water than on fresh water. In addition to their odd bills, the males are distinguished by plumage: Black Scoter all black, Surf Scoter with white head patches, White-winged Scoter with a white wing patch and a teardrop white patch behind the eye. The females have similar but more diffuse light patches.

3. THE MERGANSERS

- **Common Merganser**: the heavy, rounded greenish head of the male stands out in contrast to the brilliant white body. Looks all-white from a distance, similar to male Bufflehead. The female's beautiful chestnut head is *sharply separated* from the white neck.

- **Red-breasted Merganser**: male has a shaggy-crested green head, with white collar and gray breast. Chestnut of the female's head *shades gradually into the neck.*

- **Hooded Merganser**: male's superb, unusual hood is a sight to be enjoyed, as is similar head of the female.

While you are out enjoying and learning these ducks, you are likely to encounter some ducks that belong to minor groups not included in the chart.

The little Ruddy Duck is a member of a group called stifftails, which commonly hold their tails pointed stiffly up in the air. In winter they are rather nondescript, with a white face patch on the male and an interrupted white face patch on the female. In the spring the male's bill turns sapphire blue.

In some areas around the Gulf Coast, you also have to take into account the Whistling-Ducks (E67; W45), which are rather long-necked dabblers.

BIRDS THAT LOOK LIKE DUCKS BUT AREN'T

Some water birds that resemble ducks but are not ducks are loons, grebes, coots, and cormorants. As ducks rest on the water, they have these general shapes:

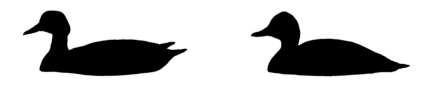

In contrast, loons (order Gaviiformes) look like this:

And grebes (order Podicipediformes) look like this:

Unless you go to the far north during the summer, the only species of loon you are likely to see on fresh water is the Common Loon, which you'll know immediately by its size and its black-and-white plumage. Other loons will most likely be on salt water, not far offshore, and in their winter plumages. Both loons and grebes have lobed feet, rather than the webbed feet of ducks, and they both dive a lot as they swim in pursuit of fish, propelled by legs that are set far back on their bodies. Although the heads of most grebes are rather angular, the little Pied-billed Grebe has a rounded head; it is a common species that you can easily learn to recognize by its size and shape.

Coots are easy: Looking out at a lake, you'll see small black bodies, perhaps hundreds of them together. Raise your binoculars, and you'll see black ducklike

birds with contrasting white bills, wagging their heads back and forth clownishly as they swim. Instead of the webbed feet of ducks, coots have lobed feet, which you may see when they come out of the water and walk around on land.

Cormorants are very easy to distinguish from other aquatic birds. They are all black and swim with their heads pointed upward, and they have long necks and long yellow, slightly hooked bills. We rarely see loons and grebes in flight, but we

often see cormorants flying around water, and frequently in large V-formation flocks. When perched, cormorants will spread their wings to dry, as do the similar Anhingas of the Deep South. Study E41 and W29, 31, for drawings and silhouettes of these forms.

EXERCISE 3-6. Study the forms of ducks, loons, and grebes. Make some notes below about their characteristic features. One hint is to pay attention to the birds' bills. Keep in mind that the flattened duck bill may not be obvious in silhouette.

_____

_____

_____

_____

_____

_____

QUIZ

After you do an exercise such as observing water birds, think about what you have seen and learned. It's an excellent way to consolidate your knowledge and make sure you really understand well. Try the following questions to test yourself. The word *kind* is meant to be ambiguous here — it could mean either a single species or a group of species.

1. A duck feeds by tipping its rear end up in the air and extending its neck downward. What kind of duck is it?

_____

2. Some black ducklike birds (maybe a raft of them) with big white bills are swimming across the lake with their heads and necks wiggling back and forth. What are they?

_____

3. A large black snaky-necked bird flies by. What is it?

_____

4. A duck takes off from the water by just barely rising over it, skittering along the surface, and gradually gaining altitude. What kind of duck is it?

_____

5. You see a duck that shows bright colors such as chestnuts and greens. Even before you can get it into focus, your mind has started to categorize it as . . . what?

_____

6. A duck at a distance on the water has a general pattern of black at the front and rear with white in between. Without knowing more about it, what category are you starting to put it in?

_____

7. A duck takes off from the water by springing directly into the air and gaining altitude quickly. What kind of duck is it?

_____

8. A duck that is all black and white is hungry. Do you expect it to dabble or dive?

    _____

9. A black-and-white duck flies by very fast, reminding you of an arrow. What is it?

    _____

    What does its bill look like and what does it use its bill for?

    _____

10. Two species of ducks each have a big patch of white on the crowns of their heads, though they look different. What are the ducks, and what is the difference in their heads?

    _____

    _____

11. A rather small bird is sitting on the water but dives frequently, so you have a hard time getting a good look at it. Its bill is like a little spear, not like a duck's bill. What do you think it is?

    _____

12. A bird way out on the water looks almost all white. It could be a gull, but if it's a duck, it's a _____ or possibly a _____.

13. A very small black duck with a white cheek patch is a _____.

14. You see a black, white, and gray duck with a large white patch on its face. It's a _____.

15. A small duck with a beautiful chestnut and green head sits on a pond, dabbling at vegetation. What is it?

NAMES AND PRONUNCIATION

Every bird species has a scientific name and at least one common name, perhaps several in different languages. The scientific name of a species — derived from Greek and Latin — is the name of its genus followed by a specific designation, the *trivial* name. For instance, the Downy Woodpecker is *Picoides pubescens* and the Hairy Woodpecker is *Picoides villosus*. Scientific names are always italicized in print; the generic name is capitalized and the trivial name is not. Generic names may change, perhaps because some ornithologists determine that the members of two genera ought to be combined, or *lumped,* into one. The Downy and Hairy Woodpeckers used to be in the genus *Dendrocopos*, while the genus *Picoides* contained the Black-backed and Three-toed Woodpeckers. Or a genus may be *split* into two or more, so some of its former members get assigned to a new genus. Lumping and splitting also happen to species, as I'll explain later. Common names sometimes change, too, usually to develop a more uniform international nomenclature, especially for broad-ranged species.

Beginners are often vexed by the pronunciation of bird names. You read a strange name in the book and wonder how to say it. As a beginner, you're naturally a little intimidated, so if you're walking with a group of more experienced people and you spot a Pileated Woodpecker, you may hesitate to call it because you wonder if you should say "*pill*-ee-ay-ted" or "*pile*-ee-ay-ted." The best answer to your puzzlement is "tomayto-tomahto," as in the old Gershwin song "Let's Call the Whole Thing Off." (Can you hear Louis Armstrong and Ella Fitzgerald singing it?) There are often alternative ways to pronounce names, just as for other words in English, depending on regional differences and family differences. You might also heed William Strunk Jr.'s advice, from Strunk and White's book *The Elements of Style*: "If you don't know how to pronounce a word, say it loud!" Your pronunciation may be as good as anyone else's. But be prepared to be corrected; some words really *can* be mispronounced. Fortunately, a reference you may want to buy anyway gives correct pronunciations of names: *The Audubon Society Encyclopedia of North American Birds* by John K. Terres. Another helpful source is Dr. Language Person's Guide to Bird Name Pronunciations at www.birds.cornell.edu/crows/birdname.htm.

SPECIES

Birding centers on species, on trying to identify species and trying to see as many species as you can, so you ought to have a clear idea of what the word *species* means. It is related to *spices,* for the medieval vendors recognized four kinds, or species, of spices, and they kept their wares in boxes divided into little compartments, with one kind of spice in each. Similarly, Linnaeus and others took the view that each kind, each species, is a distinct, unvarying entity that can be placed in its own little box, separate from all the other kinds and given its own name.

But birds are living creatures with complex lives who push their genes around in complicated ways as they reproduce — and all because of sex! Male and female birds are attracted to each other by many factors of plumage and behavior. They don't know they belong to categories that we humans call species and that they're therefore expected to mate with other individuals of the same species. But if birds don't necessarily recognize the boundaries between species that we would like to recognize, then just what the heck *is* a species? That's a difficult and controversial question, but the most generally accepted answer today was given around 1942 by the ornithologist Ernst Mayr: *A species is a group of populations that are actually or potentially capable of interbreeding with one another.* This definition applies best to animals — fortunately, the creatures we're concerned about. The way of the world is that animals of some kind reproduce with one another, generation after generation, and spread out into all the spaces where they can survive. As long as they continue to have essentially the same appearance and continue to mate with one another, we call them a single species. For instance, the species we designate American Song Sparrow, *Melospiza melodia,* consists of a lot of little streaked, brownish seed eaters. They have spread across North America into different climates and have become distinct. Song Sparrows in the temperate moist lands of eastern North America have plumage of a middle coloration, not particularly dark or light. Those adapted to hot dry desert conditions have acquired light-colored plumage, as many desert animals do. And those adapted to the relatively cool and moist lands of the coastal Pacific Northwest, reaching up the coast of British Columbia to Alaska, have acquired very dusky, rufous plumage and have become larger and larger as they have spread northward. Ornithologists recognize these differences by naming distinct *subspecies* or *races* of Song Sparrows: *Melospiza melodia melodia* in much of the East; *M. m. atlantica* along the Atlantic Coast; *M. m. fallax* in part of the desert; *M. m. morphna, M. m. merrilli,* and others in the Northwest, for a total of 39 named subspecies at this time.

But if these birds are so different, why aren't they designated different *species* of Song Sparrows? Simply because they can still *interbreed* with one another, exchanging genes to some extent across fuzzy boundaries, so they fit our conception of a single species.

What if something stopped that interbreeding? Suppose glaciation split a species into two or that some individuals flew off to an island and started a population that remained isolated from the mainland for a while. If the two populations never met, we wouldn't know if they could continue to interbreed. Populations with nonoverlapping ranges are *allopatric* (from *allo-*, "different," and *patros*, "homeland," as in *patriotism*); populations whose ranges are at least partially overlapping are *sympatric.* Closely related allopatric populations can be a puzzle. However, the separated populations could expand their ranges and become partially sympatric again. Then they would either resume interbreeding — and we would continue to call them subspecies of a single species — or they would not interbreed, and we would call them distinct species. (Or they might interbreed just a little bit, adding to our confusion.) In fact, *speciation,* the formation of new species, generally occurs when two populations become isolated from each other for a time, during which they change genetically so they don't interbreed once they meet again. We often find populations in an intermediate stage of speciation; they may be called *semispecies,* and the whole group of semispecies is a *superspecies.* Some books will note that a series of populations with formal species status are members of a superspecies, but there's no formal way of naming semispecies or superspecies.

Given bird populations in dynamic flux, ornithologists are sometimes unsure about whether two kinds of birds should be lumped as one species or split as two, and new research into the systematics of birds can change their judgments. This is why there may be differences of opinion among ornithologists and why the official list of birds changes sometimes. It reminds us that birds are organisms with complicated lives and that birding is not mere stamp collecting.

CHAPTER 4

Easy Birds First

One branch of the threefold path to birding is to start learning the easiest, most common species first. You are bound to know some of them already, and you can build on that base. The list of easiest birds will vary from one location to another and from person to person. And all of the species you learn at first may not be both easiest and most common. You might live where you can easily see a species that most people would have difficulty finding, yet it might be one of the first you can learn to recognize. On the other hand, this list doesn't include some common, easily found birds — gulls, flycatchers, sparrows — that you have to develop some sophistication to identify. I also haven't listed ducks and a few other water birds, although some of them are also among the easiest to learn.

Here are my suggestions for common species to consider learning. *I'm relying on the field guides to show you what they look like.* Also, consider again the importance of looking at silhouettes, especially as shown on the endpapers of the field guides. Many of the birds listed below, marked by a distinctive *S,* are portrayed there. Take some time to examine the silhouettes of each of these species and ask yourself just what is so distinctive about the bird that you can recognize it in this way. Look at a bluebird, for instance; its stoop-shouldered posture is obviously different from that of sparrows and cowbirds of a similar size, and you can learn to recognize this.

GREAT BLUE HERON. The biggest bird you're likely to see in its range across the United States and southern Canada. Study the pictures in your field guide, and find some GBHs to study. Get to know them. Since some other herons, as well as ibises and egrets, are common in the Southeast, especially Florida and the Gulf Coast, beginners there will have to distinguish them from GBHs; yet some of these other tall waders are distinctive enough to add to your list of easy birds.

TURKEY VULTURE. A widespread hawklike bird (a carrion eater, not a raptor), commonly seen soaring — an all-black bird with a tiny head soaring with its wings in a *dihedral,* a shallow V shape:

AMERICAN KESTREL (S). Common along country roads, this raptor often sits on wires where you can study its plumage. In flight, identified as a falcon by its *pointed wings,* compared with the more *rounded wings* of other raptors. Often hunts by hovering perhaps 20 to 40 feet off the ground before swooping down to seize a large insect or a small mammal.

RING-NECKED PHEASANT (S). Hard to miss in any grassland in a large area across the continent. Easily recognized as it explodes out of the grass and flies off, displaying a distinctive long tail.

AMERICAN COOT. As noted in chapter 3, easily distinguished from ducks.

KILLDEER (S). A brown-backed bird sporting a double necklace of stripes against its otherwise white breast; often attracts attention with its distinctive loud cry: *kill-dee, kill-dee.* The paradigm example of a shorebird, but often seen far from shores on grassy or barren land, even on the side of a highway.

SPOTTED SANDPIPER. Around lakes and streams, not as common as Killdeer. Recognized by shorebird shape and the teetering motion of its tail end, as if the bird is delicately balanced and has to keep rocking its rear up and down to stay upright. Notice its slim build, in contrast to the more robust Killdeer, and its white undersides spotted with black in breeding plumage.

MOURNING DOVE (S) AND ROCK PIGEON (FORMERLY CALLED ROCK DOVE). The most common doves (or pigeons) in North America. Recognized as doves by their erect posture, heavy bodies, and small heads. Mourning Dove has somber tan plumage, calls a plaintive *oowah coo coo coo,* differing from dark plumage and softer *coo cuck cuck cuck coo* of Rock Pigeon. Mourning Dove shows long pointed tail, contrasted with the rounded, fanlike tail of Rock Pigeon.

GREATER ROADRUNNER. Often encountered in the desert Southwest and easily recognized, even by nonbirders.

COMMON NIGHTHAWK (S). Although perched nightjars may be hard to find and identify, flying Common Nighthawks are obvious and often abundant, except for an extreme southwest area in California, Nevada, and Arizona; *crepuscular* birds, birds of the twilight, that feed in the evening high overhead, with nasal *peent, peent* calls. (Birders in some areas have noticed a severe decline, for unknown reasons.)

RUBY-THROATED HUMMINGBIRD. The only common hummer in the East. A tiny creature that hovers near flowers, almost diving into the open flower. In the West, at least 15 species of hummingbirds occur regularly, and their identification requires serious study.

BELTED KINGFISHER (S). The only kingfisher throughout most of the continent except for certain sites in Texas. Watch kingfishers. They sit still on branches over water or hover over water before diving to catch a fish. Distinctive flight — hesitating, then driving ahead in energetic bursts on powerful wingbeats, generally low over water.

WOODPECKERS. Many are easy to observe and identify. Downy and Hairy, often common in woods close to home, present a useful lesson in observing. Difference in overall size is hard to judge in the field, but compare sizes of their bills relative to heads. Downies have tiny bills, much shorter than head length; Hairy's bill is comparable to head length.

Downy   Hairy

NORTHERN FLICKER (S). Common ground feeder that flies away with a roller-coaster motion, flashing a white rump. Formerly divided into two species, Yellow-shafted in the East and Red-shafted in the West, but populations interbreed, producing birds with intermediate colors and features. Red-headed Woodpeckers: common in the East, brilliant red head and striking black-and-white wing pattern in flight. Red-bellied Woodpeckers: also common in the East, often seen at feeders. Pileated Woodpeckers: easily recognized in much of the continent. Acorn Woodpecker of the West is also obvious.

SCISSOR-TAILED FLYCATCHER (S). Common and unmistakable in the southern Great Plains.

BLUE JAY (S) AND STELLER'S JAY. Both common and well known in their areas. Study their profiles so that you'll know them even in silhouette.

SCRUB JAY (S) AND GRAY JAY. Scrub Jays of the West and Florida are formally distinct species that look very much alike. Gray Jays are common "camp robbers" across most of Canada and the mountain West of the United States; they hang around campsites waiting for a bit of food.

BLACK-BILLED MAGPIE (S). Common in the rural West; in parts of central California, it is replaced by the nearly identical Yellow-billed Magpie.

AMERICAN CROW (S). In the Southeast and along the Atlantic Coast, distinguish American Crows from Fish Crows primarily by voice, but you can master the distinction later. (Most birders in the Pacific Northwest maintain there is *no such thing* as a Northwestern Crow as a distinct species, no matter what the field guides say.) Exercise 2-8 shows you can distinguish crows from ravens by their tails in flight.

SWALLOWS (S). Commonly seen diving and swooping over lakes or meadows, often in mixed flocks of several species. Some are easily observed as they nest in colonies, under bridges or eaves of buildings, and they readily use birdhouses. Easily distinguished when perched above you, with distinctive horizontal posture (E235; W249). Leave the challenge of identification in flight for later, except perhaps for Barn Swallow, which has a deeply cut "swallowtail"; as an early exercise in learning to see birds, watch swallows circling and pick out the Barn Swallows.

CHICKADEES. Elongated little birds with tiny bills, very common at feeders or foraging among branches of a tree, often hanging upside down. Characteristic jerky, hesitating flight better observed than described. Watch chickadees enough to get used to it. You can develop your observational skills by distinguishing other species from Black-capped, the most common species across much of the continent. See field guides for field marks of Carolina Chickadees in the Southeast, Mountain and Chestnut-backed Chickadees in the West, and Boreal Chickadees in Canada.

BROWN CREEPER. Fairly common, very distinctive; literally creeps along trunks and limbs of trees, *spiraling up* tree trunks. Nuthatches, in contrast, go downward.

WHITE-BREASTED AND RED-BREASTED NUTHATCHES. Small thin-billed birds that perch upside down while foraging on tree trunks. Easily distinguished from Brown-headed Nuthatches of Southeast and Pygmy Nuthatches in parts of the West.

BLUEBIRDS (S). Beautiful and easily recognized by color and stoop-shouldered silhouette — Eastern, Western, or Mountain (note its turquoise blue) in their particular localities. Eastern and Western Bluebirds distinguished by details of plumage, a problem only in limited areas of overlap, such as New Mexico.

AMERICAN ROBIN (S). Perhaps the best-known bird in America. Study robins' posture and movements as a model for recognizing thrushes as a family.

THREE MIMIC THRUSHES (THRASHERS). In the East and Midwest, Gray Catbirds, Northern Mockingbirds (S), and Brown Thrashers seem ubiquitous. Mockingbirds are obvious across much of the United States, from southern New England to California, giving characteristic croaks and fluting whistles, flashing white wing patches in flight. Across much of the continent east of the Rockies, Catbirds and Brown Thrashers are also common. General knowledge of a thrasher's form — long sleek shape and long curved bill — helps when encountering other thrashers in the South and Southwest.

EUROPEAN STARLING (S). Raucous and extremely common almost everywhere now (to the detriment of several native American species). Attractive in breeding plumage and a good start to learning the black songbirds: starlings, cowbirds, grackles, blackbirds.

TANAGERS. Males — Scarlet and Summer in the East, Western and Hepatic in the West — are flashy, prominent. Females present identification problems best left for later (chapter 12).

TOWHEES. Distinctive plumage separates them from other sparrows; rather shy, often skulking in the bushes, but unmistakable once you see them clearly. Eastern and Spotted Towhees are largely separated geographically. Towhees and thrashers are all long-bodied, long-tailed birds, but towhees are a little stouter and have the conical bills of sparrows rather than the long thin bills of thrashers.

NORTHERN CARDINAL (S). Common and generally beloved across half the continent. In the Southwest, note their red bills (black in juveniles) to distinguish them from yellow-billed Pyrrhuloxias.

MEADOWLARKS (S). Brilliant yellow underparts; flash their white outer tail feathers as they flee across the grasslands. For now, ignore distinction between eastern and western species.

RED-WINGED AND YELLOW-HEADED BLACKBIRDS (S OF BLACKBIRDS IN GENERAL). Males obvious and unique. The large, brown, sparrow-like female Red-wings may confuse you, but find a colony of blackbirds and watch the females to start learning to distinguish them from sparrows and others.

GRACKLES (S). Over most of the continent, except the western third, Common Grackles are easy and obvious. In some parts of the South, Boat-tailed and Great-tailed Grackles are common, distinctive, hard to ignore.

GROSBEAKS. Not among the most common birds, but males are outstanding and brilliantly colored. Look at Rose-breasted and Black-headed Grosbeaks in the East and West, respectively. Roaming flocks of Evening Grosbeaks often visit bird feeders filled with sunflower seeds. Blue Grosbeaks of southern United States might be confused with bluebirds or Indigo Buntings but are separated with attention to details such as the sizes of bills and wing bars on the grosbeaks.

AMERICAN GOLDFINCH. Male has bright yellow plumage and black cap; female not easy to identify alone, but usually found in a flock with males. Distinctive roller-coaster flight pattern with repeated call, *per-chick-o-ree, per-chick-o-ree*. In the West, distinguish American from Lawrence's and Lesser Goldfinches by obvious differences in plumage.

HOUSE (ENGLISH) SPARROW (S). As fascinating as they are common. Male's rusty nape, gray cap, and black bib make him attractive and distinctive; female is very plain, with few evident field marks, and we'll distinguish it later from other North American sparrows. In the Field Exercise on p. 18, you were asked to go out and study the characteristic sparrow bills of the species.

Identify as many of these familiar common birds as you can. You might check your growing familiarity with our common birds by coming back to these photos from time to time to see how many you can recognize.

1._____

2._____

3._____

4._____   5._____

6. _____

7. _____

8. _____

9. _____

10. _____

11. _____

12. _____

13. _____

14.

15. _____

16.

17.

18.

19.

20. _____

21. _____

22._____   23._____

CHAPTER 5

Seeing Birds:
Plumage and Topography

From your lifelong habit of observing people, you know you can recognize them by many distinguishing features such as the shape of a mouth or a nose, the color of their eyes, the shape and color of their hair and how it is combed. You have now started to *see that* birds have comparable distinguishing features. In particular, you've *seen that* birds can often be recognized by the shapes of their bills, by certain features of their tails, and by their overall body shape and posture. Now it is time to start learning about other parts of a bird that may be distinctive. You must be able to *see that* a bird has a distinctive color on its throat or breast, or a distinctive superciliary stripe, or an outstanding median crown stripe. But quite obviously, it is difficult to *see that* a bird has such a feature if you are unaware that a bird *could have* a superciliary stripe or a median crown stripe. And so you must learn these surface features, features of what we call a bird's *topography* (see drawing on p. 57).

FEATHER GROUPS OF THE BODY

Feathers are a remarkable adaptation and a uniquely avian feature. They grow out of restricted regions of the skin, mostly from nine major *feather tracts*. These tracts run down the center of the head and back, at the base of the tail, along the front edges of the wings, and in other spots. In each tract, feathers grow in rows, overlapping one another like roofing shingles to form a smooth surface, such as on the breast. The bases of neighboring feathers are connected by a network of tiny muscles, allowing a bird to raise and lower its feathers to some extent. A bird can therefore take on different forms, perhaps as it fluffs out its feathers for protection against the cold. A bird's silhouette may also change considerably with its movements, as it stretches out to reach a bit of food or withdraws. These feathers create specific feather groups on the surface of the body, and each group may have a distinctive color and thus may serve as a field mark.

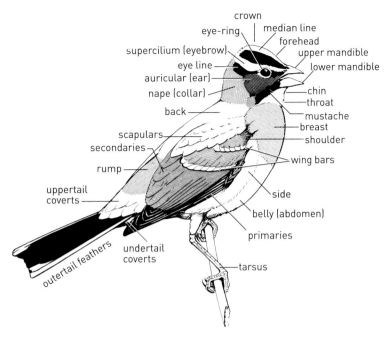

Topography of a songbird.

To begin, study the drawing, above, noting the following:

- The bird's underside (or *ventral* side) is divided into the *chin, throat, breast,* and *belly.* Behind the belly is the vent, where the intestine, excretory, and reproductive tracts all end in the anuslike cloaca. The *undertail coverts* cover the base of the tail.
- The bird's *side* is next to the breast and belly. The sides of the body just above the legs are called the *flanks,* and some birds — ducks, geese, shorebirds — have extensive flank areas.
- The bird's upper (*dorsal*) side is divided into the back of the head, the *nape* or *collar,* which extends around to the sides of the head; the upper part of the back, or *mantle*; and the lower part of the back, the *rump.* The rump, especially its lower part, is often distinctively colored. *Uppertail coverts* behind the rump cover the base of the tail above, just as the undertail coverts do below.
- The *crown* of the bird may be a separate color and may bear a *median crown stripe,* or *median line,* through its center; some species have distinct *lateral crown stripes* on each side of the median stripe (see drawing on right).

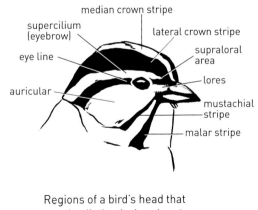

Regions of a bird's head that may be distinctively colored.

- A bird's *bill* is not properly called a "beak," and the proper terms for its parts are *upper and lower mandibles.*
- The space between the bill and the eye is called the *lores* — a singular term, even though it appears to be plural. A region just above the lores is the *supraloral area.*
- The bird may have an *eye line* going through the eye. Just above the eye, there may be a distinct stripe called an *eyebrow* or *supercilium.*
- The large *auricular*, or *ear patch*, just below and behind the eye may be distinctively colored. A distinct line at the lower edge of the auricular is called a *mustachial stripe.* A streak downward from the bill, behind the throat, is called a *malar stripe.* Some authorities use the term *submustachial stripe* for the area between the mustachial and malar stripes, but this term is not used much or is sometimes applied to the malar stripe itself.
- The eye may be surrounded by a colored circle, an *eye-ring.* Technically, an eye-ring is feathered; a ring of naked flesh around the eye is called an orbital ring. Variations in the eye-ring can make some valuable field marks, as an eye-ring may be elongated distinctively, or incomplete, with partial circles above and below the eye called *eye crescents.* Some birds, such as vireos, have an eye-ring and supraloral stripe of the same color, creating "spectacles" on the face.

After you go over these points, do the following exercises. In all of the exercises in this chapter, the objective is to learn to pay attention to details of a bird's topography and to use the correct terms in describing it — *not* to learn to identify the species. They are just used as examples. Since the descriptions of the birds in the field guide often use these terms, *don't read them first.* Use your own powers of observation and description.

EXERCISE 5-1. Describe the head of a Lark Sparrow (E299; W319), using all the correct topographic terms.

_____

_____

_____

_____

_____

_____

EXERCISE 5-2. Describe the head of a Clay-colored Sparrow (E299; W323).

_____

_____

_____

_____

EXERCISE 5-3. Describe the head, breast, and side plumage of a male Cape May Warbler (E267; W295).

_____

_____

_____

_____

EXERCISE 5-4. Although silent _Empidonax_ flycatchers are difficult to identify, what differences do you see in the heads of Least and Alder Flycatchers (E227) or in the heads of Least, Western, and Alder Flycatchers (W239, 241)?

_____

_____

_____

EXERCISE 5-5. Name an obvious field mark of Bewick's and Carolina Wrens (E241; W265).

_____

_____

_____

_____

EXERCISE 5-6. What is distinctive about the face of a Red-eyed Vireo as compared with that of a Warbling Vireo (E257; W287)?

_____

_____

EXERCISE 5-7. Describe the head, breast, and side plumage of the male Magnolia and Yellow-rumped ("Myrtle") Warblers (E265; W289). How does the Yellow-rumped "Audubon's" Warbler differ from the "Myrtle"? Then compare the females of these two species with the males and describe any differences.

_____

_____

_____

_____

_____

_____

_____

_____

_____

_____

_____

_____

_____

_____

_____

EXERCISE 5-8. If you are using the western field guide, do the same analysis for the Townsend's and Hermit Warblers (W291).

_____

_____

_____

_____

_____

_____

_____

_____

EXERCISE 5-9. What is distinctive about the head of a Northern Parula (E260)?

_____

_____

_____

EXERCISE 5-10. Describe the head patterns of the adult White-crowned, White-throated, and Golden-crowned Sparrows (E295; W317). Later, we will touch on the question of recognizing these three as _Zonotrichia_ sparrows, but if you see such a bird in the field, and you can't get a good look at the bird's throat and bill, what feature or features will you try to notice first before the bird flies away?

_____

_____

_____

_____

EXERCISE 5-11. How does the head of a Northern Goshawk differ from that of a Cooper's Hawk (E99; W173)?

_____

_____

_____

EXERCISE 5-12. Compare the heads of Nashville, Connecticut, and Mourning Warblers (E275) or of Nashville, Connecticut, MacGillivray's, and Mourning Warblers (W299). Notice that the term *hood* is useful for the dark head, chin, throat, and upper breast of birds like these.

_____

_____

THE WING AND BACK AREA

The drawing below shows the feather topography of a bird's wing. Note particularly the *wrist* — the bend in the wing — and the *wing linings*, which contrast with the *flight feathers* — the *primaries* and *secondaries* — also called *remiges* (singular *remex*). Most birds have 10 primaries, although some passerines have

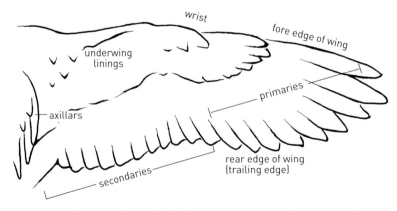

General surface structure of a bird's wing, as seen on the undersurface.

only 9 and some larger birds have 16 or 18. The wing typically has 9 secondaries; the 3 innermost secondaries, called *tertials*, may be distinct anatomically and colored differently. It may be useful to turn to the plates of gulls in flight, especially E179 or W93, and look at their wings. The bend of the wing at the wrist marks the line between the primaries and secondaries.

EXERCISE 5-13. If a gull has black wingtips (E179; W93), which feathers have that color?

Primaries and secondaries are distinguished by their attachment to the bones of the wing, which you can understand easily by comparing them to your own hand and arm bones. You have a large *humerus* in your upper arm, the paired *radius* and *ulna* in your lower arm (the radius is the bone on the same side as your thumb), several small *carpals* in your wrist, 5 *metacarpals* extending through your hand to the base of each finger, and then 3 *phalanges* in each finger, except for your thumb, which has only 2. As birds evolved from ancestral reptiles, their wrist and hand structure was severely reduced to a few small phalanges and a long bone called the *metacarpus,* made of the ancestral metacarpals condensed into one. The primaries are attached to this remnant of the hand and wrist, mostly to the metacarpus; the secondaries are attached to the ulna; and the humerus is somewhat buried inside the body and has no feathers attached.

LOOKING AT WINGS

The bases of the flight feathers are covered by smaller feathers called *coverts.* A row of *greater coverts* lies directly over the flight feathers, then rows of *median coverts,* and finally smaller *lesser coverts.* There are both upperwing coverts and underwing coverts, and some birds, such as hawks and shorebirds, have distinctively colored and patterned underwing coverts. The base of the wing on the upper side is covered by *scapulars.*

The folded wings of birds may bear important field marks, which you should look for as you are making a mental inventory of field marks. The most common features — aside from no marks at all — are *wing bars* (shown on p. 57) on the edges of the coverts. But wing markings vary considerably, from slight suggestions of bars to strong, obvious bars to patches of various kinds. To start developing your awareness of wing markings, do the following exercises.

EXERCISE 5-14. On E267 or W295, examine the wings of all the male birds shown and describe the wing patterns.

_____

_____

_____

_____

_____

EXERCISE 5-15. On E297 or W321, examine the wings of the adult sparrows and describe any differences you see in the wing patterns. What happens to the wings of Chipping Sparrows as they change from juveniles to adults or as they change from winter to breeding plumage?

_____

_____

_____

_____

_____

EXERCISE 5-16. The three common thrashers — Brown Thrasher, Gray Catbird, and Northern Mockingbird (E249; W271) — are among the birds you can learn early. How do their wings differ?

_____

_____

_____

_____

EXERCISE 5-17. E225 or W237 shows that the Eastern Phoebe and the Eastern or Western Wood-Pewees are very similar, but how do their wing patterns distinguish them?

_____

_____

_____

_____

EXERCISE 5-18. Baltimore and Bullock's Orioles (E317; W313) are very similar and for a time were considered a single species. How do the wings of the males differ?

_____

_____

_____

_____

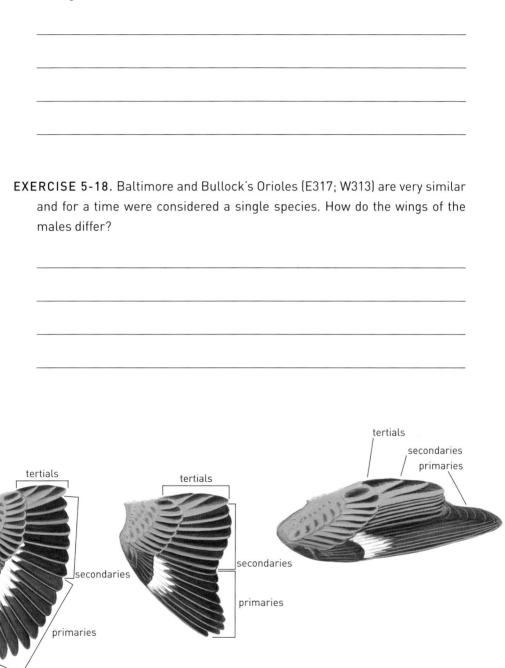

How a bird's wing folds. The base of the wing is covered by rows of coverts.

Now look at p. 65 to see how the wing folds up. This is David Sibley's painting of the wing of a passerine (a Black-throated Blue Warbler), showing that the primaries and secondaries wind up largely covered by other feathers and that the tertials particularly are quite visible. But the folded wing varies considerably from order to order. In some, such as herons and ducks, much of the area we can see on the folded wing is covered by coverts and tertials, with hardly any of the primaries visible at all.

If you hold your arms out to the sides, making "wings," as children sometimes do, you'll naturally aim your thumbs forward. Although birds don't have any thumbs left, they effectively hold their wings in the same position, because some of their flight feathers (secondaries) are attached to the ulna, opposite the thumb, which must be on the trailing edge. To fold its wings, the bird bends them at both the elbow and wrist, just as you do; now bring your "wings" onto your back, as if you were folding them, and you'll make your thumbs touch, so your imaginary feathers stay at your side. If you were really a bird folding your wings, the feathers that are so nicely spread out in flight would fold together into a compact stack. The figure shows how this happens and what flight feathers are visible when a bird is perched. The primaries are underneath, extending toward the tail; the secondaries lie over them, and the tertials over the secondaries.

Look at the *standing* gulls on E175, 179, or W91, especially at the birds in adult plumage where you can easily see the black tips on the primaries in contrast to the gray secondaries. Now you can see that when the wing is folded, virtually the only parts of the primaries that are still visible are those black tips, extending beyond the secondaries. The distance they extend, called the *primary extension,* is often helpful in identifying a bird. Finally, notice the tail feathers, below the wings on these gulls. When looking at a perched bird, it is important to know if you are looking at the wings or the tail, and which is longer. The wings of these gulls clearly extend past the tail. The tails of passerines generally extend way beyond their wingtips, but look at perched swallows. The relative lengths of the tail and wings is important in identifying some shorebirds.

MOLTS AND PLUMAGES

A *plumage* is the set of feathers a bird is wearing at any time. Birds change their plumages like sets of clothes as they mature from hatchlings to adults. Then as adults they go through a series of annual molts. Feathers get lost and wear out, so regularly replacing old feathers is an important adaptation for keeping a bird in top physical condition. But there is considerable variation across the orders of birds in the number of molts per year and their details. As you mature in birding, you'll learn to recognize more birds in their various plumages.

Feathers grow out of follicles in the skin, much like our hair follicles. An emerging feather soon begins to acquire its mature form, starting at its tip, and then elongates rapidly to its final length and pushes the old feather out of the follicle. Molting generally doesn't interfere with a bird's essential activities; for instance, adult birds typically molt after breeding, not during the critical time when they are raising and protecting their young. Some birds, however, such as ducks, grebes, and pelicans, molt all their feathers during one brief period and for a short time are unable to fly.

Many species have a plumage during their spring and summer breeding season that differs from their nonbreeding plumage, so ornithologists and birders in Northern Hemisphere regions have generally described plumages with the *life year system* as breeding or nonbreeding, summer or winter. In this system, a newly hatched bird has a *natal plumage,* which may be the fuzzy, downy coat of chicks and ducklings or only a few scattered down feathers. Over the next few weeks, the baby bird quickly grows new feathers in preparation for its first flight and is called a *juvenile.* During the following fall and winter it acquires its *first-winter* plumage, followed during the spring and summer by its *first-summer* plumage. It then undergoes a complete molt, which may produce *adult* or *definitive* plumage; if the plumage acquired then is still not fully adult, the bird is said to have its *second-winter plumage,* followed by *second-summer plumage,* and so on. In the field guides, many species are shown in *immature* plumages, which simply means one that differs significantly from a fully adult plumage. The time needed to acquire adult plumage varies enormously with species; the large gulls take three or four years, small passerines less than a year.

Some birds acquire their breeding plumage by the wearing away of feather tips rather than by a distinct molt. In this way, birds such as House Sparrows, European Starlings, and meadowlarks lose their dull winter plumage and reveal their bright spring colors.

Ornithologists increasingly use a system devised in 1959 by Philip Humphrey and Kenneth Parkes. By emphasizing molt, which can occur at any season, the Humphrey-Parkes system divorces the appearance of a bird from seasons and can be used with birds of any region. It distinguishes *basic plumage* — the plumage a bird wears during most of the year, outside of its breeding season — from *alternate plumage,* the adornments it may acquire temporarily during breeding. Basic plumage is acquired during a complete molt of all feathers, called the *prebasic molt*; if a bird has an alternate plumage, it is acquired by partial replacement of only some feathers during the *prealternate molt.* The further details get complicated and are more than beginners need to know.

SUPPLEMENTARY EXERCISE

For practice in using topographic terms, look at the plates of similar birds, such as the wood warblers, and write descriptions of their plumages.

CHAPTER 6

Eight Passerine Families

Now it's time to focus on some major families of passerines, the birds you'll en-counter most often in most environments. In listing common, easy birds, we've already met some families of passerines that stand out: chickadees (Paridae), nuthatches (Sittidae), some of the thrashers (Mimidae), and several of the corvids (Corvidae) — jays, crows, and magpies. Here we'll move on to eight families, most of which include many species that you'll learn gradually. The idea here is first to learn to recognize them as families before tackling individual species, and to keep developing a vocabulary of bird *gestalts*. You can learn to recognize the birds in each of these families from a distance just by their jizz, particularly by their behavior. Some of them may be characterized as "nervous": constantly on the move, hunting for insects and other small animals, moving quickly to grab any morsel of food. In contrast, other passerines are placid: they sit still quite a lot or move rather slowly and deliberately.

TYRANT FLYCATCHERS (TYRANNIDAE)

Small to medium-sized birds with high crowns and substantial bills. They sit *upright and very still* on an exposed perch, perhaps moving only their heads. Some other birds may sit in similar ways, but a bird in that pose is likely to be a fly-catcher, and that should be one of the first things that comes to mind. Watch the bird for a while. If it darts out to catch an insect — which you prob-ably can't see — and returns to the same perch or one nearby, it is probably a flycatcher. Other passerines, such as waxwings, also hawk insects, but they tend to behave differently. A bluebird, for instance, is more likely to drop down on an insect and eat it on the ground before returning to its perch, and a perched bluebird presents a very different silhouette.

KINGLETS (REGULIDAE)

Tiny, short, very nervous birds with tiny bills. Kinglets and chickadees are sprites that play among the trees, often high in the trees, and may feed acrobatically, upside down. Chickadees, however, are more elongated and kinglets are shorter. Kinglets also mark themselves by their constant wing flicking, the Ruby-crowned more than the Golden-
crowned. Kinglets live mostly in conifers (spruces, firs, pines), though in the winter they forage in all kinds of trees. And in winter we commonly see mixed flocks of chickadees, kinglets, and Yellow-rumped Warblers.

THRUSHES (TURDIDAE)

Medium-sized birds with slender but strong bills adapted for the variety of foods they eat — fruits, worms, other small animals — neither the conical bill of a seed eater nor the tiny, thin bill of an insect eater. Thrushes are among the most distinctive, easily recognized families, as exemplified by American Robins. (Bluebirds are thrushes, too, but their posture is different, and they fly-catch as described above, so let's leave them
aside. Generalizations can be so perilous!) A thrush stands upright, an attitude that seems to express confidence and alertness, almost fearlessness. When moving over the ground, sometimes running rather than hopping, it is alert for a bit of food and often pauses, cocking its head to one side or the other. When flushed, it generally flies up onto the branch of a tree and stands motionless.

SPARROWS (EMBERIZIDAE)

Small to medium-sized birds with conical seed-eating bills; they move deliberately but not nervously. Sparrows, on the whole, are birds of the ground or of grasses and other plants close to the ground, where they find their food, mostly seeds. A sparrow may cling to a plant stalk as it eats the nearby seeds, or it may move slowly over the ground. Sparrows are gleaners. They find the residue of food left by other animals. Most sparrows are distinguished by their plumages of brown, black, gray,

white, and rust. (Towhees are in the sparrow family, but they have quite different plumage.) North American buntings and finches, often brightly colored birds, have bills like sparrows but are classified in other families. Beginners may find sparrows hard to identify, so we take up the whole family in chapter 16.

WRENS (TROGLODYTIDAE)

Small, brownish "sprightly" birds: energetic, active, seldom still. This distinguishes them from other small brown birds that are more stolid and slow moving. Wrens share the ground and low vegetation with sparrows, but their bills are long, thin, and slightly curved, good for fishing insects and other small invertebrates out of crevices and holes. The way they hold their tails erect is most distinctive.

WOOD WARBLERS (PARULIDAE)

The American Wood Warblers have been called the butterflies of the bird world because of their wonderful variety of bright colors, which you can see by browsing the plates of warblers in a field guide. Most warblers have some yellow color, a point that should become a part of your overall warbler gestalt. They are among the most nervous-acting of birds, as they actively move through a woodland, darting from branch to branch, tree to tree, making them

hard to observe when the trees are leafed out. Birders in the East and Midwest are sometimes treated to "warbler waves," when hundreds or thousands of these little birds, of many species, move through the woods in spring migration, largely before the trees are fully leafed out. This is the best time to see warblers and learn to identify them. During the fall migration, many warblers — especially females and immature birds — have plain olive and yellow plumages, which Peterson treats specially in the plates of confusing fall warblers (E279, 281). The warblers — and the vireos in the next family — are all small insect eaters, but the distinction between them is a bit subtle, and mastering it may require considerable observation time.

VIREOS (VIREONIDAE)

Vireos are small gray, olive, and yellowish birds, slightly larger than warblers (though that may be hard to see) and with heavier, slightly curved bills that have slight hooks at the end, which they use for feeding on insects and fruit. Vireos move more sedately than warblers, more deliberately; when a vireo perches, it usually remains still for a short time, but warblers move incessantly. Vireos also have duller plumages, almost always with gray or olive backs and slightly yellow undersides. Notice that the vireo species are usefully divided into those that have wing bars and those that do not. Most of them also have strong eyebrow lines or "spectacles" made by eye-rings combined with supraloral stripes.

BLACKBIRDS AND RELATIVES (ICTERIDAE)

Icterids are medium-sized birds, generally sleek and elongated, with long, sharp, curved bills, especially with curved upper mandibles. Meadowlarks have the longest, sharpest bills, Bobolinks and cowbirds shorter, more sparrowlike bills. Several of the icterids (Redwinged and Yellow-headed Blackbirds, grackles, and meadowlarks) are on the list of

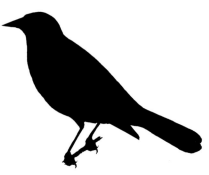

common, easy birds. The family also includes the somber, all-black blackbirds and the spectacular orioles, with their dazzling orange and black or yellow and black plumage. Most icterids give a long slim impression; the chunky little meadowlarks are an exception.

QUIZ

What families introduced in this chapter do these birds belong to?

1. _____

2. _____

3. _____

4. _____

5. _____

6. _____

7. _____   8. _____

9. _____   10. _____

11. _____   12. _____

Note: The following questions refer to birds in the families introduced here as well as groups of birds introduced in earlier chapters. You may have to turn back to find some of those other groups.

13. A small bird is standing on a lawn so far away that you can hardly see its shape. It stands still for a few seconds, runs a few feet, stands still again, and then repeats this behavior, occasionally pecking at the grass. What family does it belong to?

_____

14. A small elongated bird is hanging upside down in a fir tree, pecking at a cone. What kind of bird is it?

_____

15. In a weedy field, a small brownish bird is clinging to a weed stalk and picking out seeds. What kind of bird is it?

_____

16. You have just walked into a woodland in the eastern United States. Suddenly a bird with this shape comes and sits on a branch nearby. What is it?

_____

17. A very small bird with a short thin bill is flitting around in the branches of a tree, hopping quickly from branch to branch. It keeps flashing its wings out. What is it?

_____

18. As you are looking down at a marsh, a small bird waddles out of the reeds and walks around in the shallow water. It walks in a bent-over position, with its tail somewhat up in the air and its long curved bill pointed downward. What is it?

_____

19. You walk out the back door of your house and see a small brown bird moving stealthily among the plants. It has a moderately long, somewhat curved bill and is pointing its tail up in the air. What is it?

_____

20. A small bird is perched at the top of an exposed tree branch. It just sits there, hardly moving. Whoops — suddenly it darts out into the air, turns around, and returns to its perch. What is it most likely to be?

_____

21. A medium-sized bird, blue above and white below, sits on a branch over a quiet lake. Suddenly it takes flight, dives into the lake, and returns to its perch. What is it?

_____

22. A small bird with a thin bill is searching actively through the foliage of a bush, showing a lot of yellow color. What is it most likely to be?

_____

23. Walking through a quiet woodland, you become aware of the sound of something pecking or hammering lightly on a tree. Then you see that the sound is coming from a small black-and-white bird clinging to the side of a branch. What is it?

_____

24. A small bird with a thin bill is searching actively through the foliage of a bush. It has an overall yellowish color and looks like it is wearing yellow eyeglasses. What is it?

_____

25. You are standing on the rocky coastline of either New England or Alaska, looking at thousands of birds that are black above and white below. What general kind are they?

_____

CHAPTER 7

Watching Birds in Flight

We commonly see birds in flight, and many plates in the field guides are devoted to their critical features. You'll find it useful to become familiar with the flight of the most common birds in your home area. Two aspects of watching birds in flight are seeing patterns of movement and seeing details of shape and topography. We'll begin with the first one, which requires you to go out and observe some common birds.

MOVEMENT AND JIZZ

Birds fly with many distinct patterns. Experts recognize species to a large extent by their flight, an important aspect of their jizz, and you'll want to start learning this yourself on your way to expertise; since the field guides emphasize birds' appearance and vocalization, you may be surprised at how unique and telling patterns of flight can be. Some birds fly with regular, steady beats. Others are very irregular. Some species glide with their wings spread, and others fold their wings for intervals as they glide, like missiles. We can't catalog this information for every species, but *Pete Dunne's Essential Field Guide Companion* focuses a lot on flight, and you'll find it a truly useful guide as you become more familiar with North American birds. Here are a few exercises to start you on the path to watching flight critically.

In the field exercises that follow, the species I'm suggesting you observe are common and widespread, so they should not be difficult to find. If you do need help locating these birds, check the range maps and habitat descriptions in your field guide.

FIELD EXERCISES

One of the first lessons you can teach yourself is about the relationship between a bird's size and the speed of its movements, especially its flight. In general, larger birds flap their wings more slowly, although size and speed are not strictly correlated. As one extreme, try to find a Great Blue Heron flying (or one of the other large herons or egrets, if you live where they are common). Notice that the wings pump ponderously slowly; the bird has very high *wing-loading*, the ratio of its mass to the surface area of its wings. Per gram of body mass, the heron requires more energy to move around than does a smaller bird, and it simply can't fly with the rapid wing movements of little birds.

Observe the depth of a bird's wingbeat. A bird's wings may be beating so fast that they are just a blur, but that blur shows the *envelope* of movement. Particularly when you watch a bird flying away from you for a few seconds, you can tell whether the wings move deeply, over a wide arc, or shallowly, over a narrow arc:

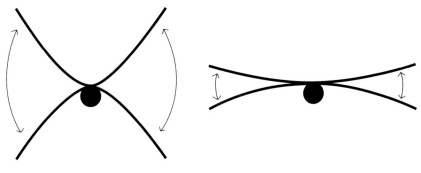

Deep wingbeat   Shallow wingbeat

Pigeons are good subjects for this exercise, although many other birds will do; this is a point to watch for on all birds in flight. Observe as many birds as you can, and make notes about the pattern of wingbeat for each of them.

For birds of intermediate size, let's concentrate on some common birds, the corvids — the crows, jays, and their relatives. Crows are good subjects for study, since we see them almost everywhere. They're mostly American Crows, *Corvus brachyrhynchos*, but Fish Crows or other species will also do. All North American crows are much the same in this respect.

(1) Watch some crows in regular, straight flight, not fighting a strong wind or changing their direction much. Study their flight. Since crows are so common, and their flight is so steady and regular, you might use them as a kind of baseline model of bird flight to compare other birds against. How does the wingbeat rate compare to that of a Great Blue Heron?

(2) Now try to watch some crows fighting a moderate to strong wind or trying to change their direction. Does their flight look ragged or sloppy? Notice how the birds look under various conditions and try to commit the pattern to memory as you continue to see crows on your outings.

(3) While you're studying crows, you might as well take a close look at them when they are perched on a tree. Look at them from up close as well as from various distances. As you get farther from the tree, the crows increasingly become black spots, but get a sense of the size of those spots in relation to the tree, to its leaves, and to other objects around. You'll see similar black spots of different sizes, especially starlings and blackbirds; try to distinguish them at a distance by their sizes. Also, watch some crows while they are calling from the limb of a tree; a calling crow stretches its body out in an elongated shape, pumping back and forth as it calls; it helps to become familiar with crows in this posture.

Next, turn your attention to jays — Blue Jays in the East, Steller's Jays in the West. They are among the easiest birds to identify; try to see them at a moderate distance when they are little more than silhouettes, to become familiar with their elongated bodies and distinctively crested heads. (Scrub Jays are also good subjects, though of course they don't have crested heads.) Then watch some jays flying. This will be a lesson in noticing flight patterns and shapes at a distance. To my eyes, the elongated tails of Steller's Jays in the distance are so narrow where they meet the body as to look hardly attached. The jay's flight pattern is distinctive: It flaps a few times and then sails a little, flaps a few times and sails a little. Each species of jay has a particular pattern, and the more you can observe these distinctions, the better off you'll be. Spend as much time as you can watching jays and becoming familiar with the shape of their bodies and the way they fly. You'll find that with a little practice, you can identify a bird as a jay even from afar.

Find some European Starlings. Small flocks of starlings are common around any urban or suburban environment, especially in the fall and winter. Watch starlings fly, paying particular attention to their wings. Starlings in flight are often described as being very *triangular,* and their short, triangular wings are distinctive. Their wings may also give you an impression of being transparent; they are flapping so fast that it looks as though you can see the sky through them.

Find some Northern Flickers, American Goldfinches, or both. The lesson here is about *undulating* flight, flight with a roller-coaster motion. You will probably encounter a flicker feeding on the ground, and it will fly away with its body rising and falling in a wavy motion. (Although you should avoid disturbing birds, especially while they are feeding, you will inevitably provoke some into flight, and you should take the opportunity to study them.) The bird will flash its white rump patch at you, and it's good to start recognizing that as a field mark, since other woodpeckers (Red-bellied Woodpeckers and most sapsuckers, for instance) and several other species of birds also have prominent rump or tail patches.

Speaking of woodpeckers, pay attention to their flight patterns. Although each species has its own way of flying, as a group they tend to have undulating flight with a lot of gliding, often closed-wing gliding.

Goldfinches also exhibit undulating flight, and they move more quickly. An American Goldfinch often repeats its flight call, *per-chick'-o-ree, per-chick'-o-ree*, in rhythmic accompaniment to its flight, with a loud *chick* at the peak of each wave.

Find a Belted Kingfisher and watch it fly over water. Write a description of what you see. Are its wingbeats deep or shallow? Some adjectives that may come to mind include *hesitant, jerky*, and *controlled*. Which of these fits this species? Can you think of others? Study the bird and try to describe it so its flight becomes strongly imprinted on your memory.

WING SHAPE

A bird's wings folded at rest reveal little about their shape and coloration when extended in flight, and the folded wings may cover up important field marks such as colorful wing linings or rump patches that are often so critical to making an identification. A bird reveals these features as it takes flight. A flying bird may also show its tail more clearly than when it's at rest, and a startled bird flying away from you may provide the glimpse of its tail that you need to see a critical field mark.

The shape of a bird's wings in flight is one of its distinctive and most easily seen features. Peterson emphasized this with the back endpaper silhouettes in the eastern guide; unfortunately, these aren't used in the western guide, so please direct your attention to specific plates. If you have the eastern guide, look at the back endpaper. A bird's wings, especially its wingtips, have one of two general shapes. What are they? _____ or _____.

If you're not sure your answer is the same as mine, let me point you to birds that show these two classes of wing shapes.

Class 1: ducks, gulls, sandpipers, swallows
Class 2: grouse and pheasants, woodpeckers, mockingbirds, shrikes

The general categories are *pointed* and *rounded,* and the larger birds with rounded wingtips have well-separated primary feathers at their tips. The difference between the two classes is often critical; look at the general distinctions among classes of diurnal birds of prey (hawks) on E94–95 or W192–96. Look at the differences between buteos and accipiters, with their rounded wings, and falcons, with their pointed wings. As you learn to identify these birds, this wing shape will be one of the first points to notice, especially when they are overhead, seen against a bright sky.

Rounded and pointed wings have different aerodynamic and behavioral meanings. Birds with rounded wings can fly short distances quickly and maneuver with remarkable agility. This is especially true if they also have long tails; the hawks called accipiters, for instance, can negotiate the spaces between branches in a dense woodland at breakneck speed as they pursue their prey, generally small birds. Birds with pointed wings are better suited to gliding for long distances, with little or no flapping.

FIELD EXERCISES

Speaking of gliding, find some gulls and watch them as they glide. Look at the shape of their wings and describe their wings and their behavior.

This may be more difficult to do, but game birds such as Ring-necked Pheasants and Northern Bobwhites are common in many places, and you will often flush them — explosively! — as you walk across a grassy field. If you encounter one of them, look at the bird's wings, even if they are moving so fast as to be blurred. Notice how their short, rounded shape allows these birds to fly rapidly and change direction quickly.

No one can predict what birds you're likely to see flying, but in general you'll increase your birding skill enormously by noticing the particulars of how each species flies and adding it to your conception of the bird's jizz. We have already noted the shapes of various hawks in flight, and when we take up the hawks in chapter 13 we'll pay a lot of attention to their shapes, their ways of moving, and their wing patterns.

CHAPTER 8

Diagnosing a Group of Birds

Some inexperienced birders are standing on the boardwalk in my local wildlife refuge with a field guide open, desperately turning pages and trying to match a bird they've seen in the bush with one of the pictures. This is one of the saddest sights I encounter in the field. Too often, the beginners fail, and they wind up frustrated and convinced that they'll never succeed at this arcane business of birding. The problem is that they're studying the book at the wrong time — while they are in the field, rather than at home. If you hope to learn to identify birds, it is essential to study the book *before* you go into the field, to prepare yourself for what you might see.

"What you might see." This course of study has so far emphasized seeing birds in specific ways, and you've learned that seeing is largely a matter of *seeing that* a bird has certain specific features: that its body has a certain form, that it has a bill of this shape rather than that shape, a tail with a certain form and coloration, or that it has various marks, stripes, and patches of color on named areas all over its body. So far I've been trying to direct you toward learning to see all these particulars by choosing a few examples from the hundreds of North American birds. Now it is time for you to take the next step and select for yourself the features of a group of birds that are most important to see.

Every spring, millions of birds that have been wintering in South and Central America migrate northward, and many of them fly across the Gulf of Mexico. When they reach the Gulf Coast they are exhausted, and they fall out on the land to replenish their energy in preparation for the next leg of their journey across the rest of the continent. The Gulf Coast is therefore a marvelous place for spring birding, and High Island, Texas, is one of the best localities. One wonderful spring day at High Island, I encountered a group of British birders. As I listened to them excitedly discussing their observations, it became obvious that they were very well prepared. I mentioned this to one of them, and he said, "Did you think we'd come all this way without being prepared for the birds we might see in America?" I suppressed the temptation to say that I was afraid many American birders would not prepare properly for a similar birding trip to Europe. He went on to say that his birding group met once a week, and each time they studied the key field marks and worked to become familiar with a different group of North American birds. So they were eminently well prepared for their trip, and I'm sure they had a wonderful time.

Although I don't know exactly how those British birders analyzed each group of birds, their general course of action holds a lesson for all of us. To be successful as a birder, you have to study the field guides at home to prepare yourself, especially to see each group of birds. This is the course of study we've been following: first, becoming more familiar with orders and families, especially with the families of passerines outlined in chapter 6, and then starting to learn the most common, easiest birds in your area. Along the way, you have probably been learning to recognize outstanding eastern birds such as Northern Cardinals, Scarlet Tanagers, and Baltimore Orioles or western birds such as Western Tanagers and Bullock's Orioles. You don't need any particular regime of studying to learn to recognize them — the males, at least. But many plates in the field guides show several birds that look very similar, noting the field marks that separate them. How do you make use of this information? It's hard to make much progress by just looking at the pictures casually in the book and trying to memorize field marks. (Also, the field guide may point out several important field marks, but you may have only a few seconds to observe a bird — which marks are most important to see in that time?) To focus your studying, you often need a more active, personal method. You need to do a diagnosis.

Diagnosing a bird group means analyzing their features so you will know what to look for when you're in the field. A good diagnosis will help you focus on the essential points needed to distinguish one species from another. However, doing a diagnosis is basically a personal activity; don't think of the end product of your work as an analysis you could publish or give to someone else to use, because the *process* is really most important, and you may eventually forget the product anyway. Someone else's diagnosis might be distinctly different, and that's okay, because you are both using the process for learning. (For this reason, the answers to exercises that call on you to do a diagnosis generally will just call attention to important characteristics rather than giving a single correct answer.)

For example, suppose you live in my area, coastal Washington. You recognize wrens as a family, and you want to be able to identify the wrens you see in the field. By paying close attention to the field marks of the wrens in the field guide (W265), you might conclude that one feature to focus on is the prominent white eyebrow stripe on some wrens, so in the field you will want to *see if* a bird has such a stripe. (*Seeing if* is just a grammatical variation on *seeing that*.) Suppose it does; then it is either a Marsh Wren or a Bewick's Wren. Now, what can you look for to distinguish them? Ah, the Marsh Wren has prominent white stripes on the back; Bewick's does not. But suppose the bird has no white eyebrow stripe; then it is either a House Wren or a Winter Wren. The Winter Wren is small and stubby-tailed, while the House Wren is slim with a long tail. So your diagnosis can be summarized like this:

White eyebrow stripe?

1. Yes. White stripes on back?
   a. Yes: *Marsh*
   b. No: *Bewick's*

2. No. Look at the tail.
   a. Very small and stubby-tailed: *Winter*
   b. Larger, slim, long-tailed: *House*

The outline of this diagnosis has the form of a *key,* a device used in many books for identifying species. A key to a group of wildflowers, for instance, may require you to look step by step at features such as the shape and arrangement of leaves, the number of petals in a flower, the arrangement of stamens and pistils in a flower, and other anatomical details. We *key out* a specimen by making a series of yes-or-no decisions about its features. In diagnosing birds, it is sometimes useful to have a choice among three or more possibilities; don't feel you have to restrict yourself to binary decisions.

Winnowing or *sieving* are also good metaphors for this procedure. You pass a group of birds through a series of mental sieves that either identify a species or eliminate some that don't have the right features, so step by step you focus on the features of the bird at hand.

In this diagnosis we have focused on the bird's morphology only. In your growing sophistication, you will see that Marsh Wrens are to be expected only in wet marshy habitats and Winter Wrens in the undergrowth of coniferous or mixed-coniferous forests, and you will add information about their distinctive calls. Here I'm restricting the idea of diagnosis to appearance, but you could perfectly well add diagnostic features of any kind.

Now it's time for you to develop some diagnoses of your own. In the later chapters of this book, where we examine some of the more difficult birds, I'll ask you to do several diagnoses. Here are a few preliminary exercises to help you get used to the idea. (And remember that your diagnoses may differ from those given in the answers.)

EXERCISE 8-1. This is a simple one: diagnose the Red and White-winged Crossbills (E285; W341).

_____

_____

EXERCISE 8-2. Diagnose the male blue finches: Blue Grosbeak; Indigo, Lazuli, and Blue Buntings (E289).

_____

_____

_____

_____

_____

EXERCISE 8-3. Do a diagnosis of the shrikes (E254; W281).

_____

_____

_____

_____

_____

EXERCISE 8-4. Diagnose the vireos without wing bars. For the East (E257), this means Red-eyed, Black-whiskered, Warbling, and Philadelphia Vireos. For the West (W287), this means Red-eyed, Gray, Warbling, and Philadelphia Vireos. Of course, include the Yellow-green Vireo if you wish, but it's a specialty of a few spots along the Mexican border.

_____

_____

EXERCISE 8-5. Do a diagnosis of flying swallows. They can be hard to follow, and you may get only a flash of a part as the bird swoops past. But even on a rapidly moving bird you can catch some of the features of swallows perched overhead (E235; W249), and you can see other features of plumage and shape that are most visible when a bird is flying, as shown in the Peterson guide. Deal with Barn, Bank, Tree (adult only), Rough-winged, Violet-green, Cliff, and Purple Martin.

Suggestion: Look first for the most outstanding features that will separate out one or a few.

EXERCISE 8-6. Four western zebra-backed woodpeckers — Nuttall's, Ladder-backed, Gila, and Golden-fronted (W229) — are separated largely by range and habitat, but it's useful to diagnose them anyway, perhaps including range or habitat in your diagnosis.

EXERCISE 8-7. This is a somewhat specialized problem for western birders, but you might find it useful for practice even if you don't live in the West. Do a diagnosis of some common western Washington summer warblers: Yellow, Orange-crowned, Yellow-rumped, Black-throated Gray, Wilson's, MacGillivray's, and Common Yellowthroat.

First challenge. Do this for males only, which is relatively easy.

Second challenge. Consider both males and females, since you'll see both in the field. This will be a little tougher. (Note: The symbol for male is ♂ ["the arrow and shield of Mars"] and for female is ♀ ["the mirror of Venus"].)

_____

_____

_____

_____

_____

_____

_____

_____

CHAPTER 9

Vocalizations

The Compleat Birder pays as much attention to bird sounds as to their appearance, perhaps even more. Experts locate nine out of ten birds by their calls and songs, and they also identify many birds in this way. Sometimes a bird's voice is the only way to know it is present. Walking through a dense woodland, you will hear many bird voices coming from all directions, while your eyes can focus on only a small area at one time and the birds are often hidden behind leaves or in the treetops. You generally can't wade out into a marsh, but you can hear the calls of birds there. Also, voice is the only way out of several birding conundrums, the way to clearly distinguish one species from another. Look, for instance, at the analysis of *Empidonax* flycatchers (E227; W239), which are so similar that silent birds often must be recorded simply as "*Empidonax* species." If beginners have difficulty learning voices, I think it is because most people find it harder in general to remember sounds than to remember things they see. A second issue in dealing with voice is that many people have lost some ability to hear. Our society is noisy. Our ears are assaulted by the noises of civilization — automobile engines, home appliances, chain saws, jackhammers, rock music — and a substantial portion of our population has suffered some hearing loss. Some of the decline in hearing is due to age, although anthropologists have noted that elderly members of isolated tribes in natural, quiet environments can hear as well as their young people can. Some decline results from disease and injury. Birders who want to get the maximum pleasure from their pastime and who aspire to expertise need to guard their ears.

TYPES OF BIRD VOCALIZATIONS

All birds produce some characteristic sounds, not just songs — the quacks of ducks, the cries of gulls, the hooting of owls. The rhythms of woodpeckers drumming on trees are distinctive, too, even if they aren't strictly vocalizations. Many of these sounds are familiar, and they may not be very species specific. The voices that most birders are concerned about — and which may be the most troubling — are generally those of passerines, specifically the songbirds. All birds have a vocal apparatus, the *syrinx,* at the base of the trachea; the order Passeriformes has two suborders, the oscines and suboscines, and the syrinx of oscines has a complex arrangement of muscles that control its vibrating membranes. Songbirds produce two types of vocalizations: calls and songs. Calls are brief vocalizations, perhaps only single notes, used to express aggression, warn about a danger, seek a companion, or keep a flock together. Songs are the more elaborate, more musical vocalizations that are produced almost exclusively by males to announce their territorial claims and to attract mates. Thus birds' vocalizations have important social functions, and many species that have been studied carefully sing a repertoire of distinct calls and songs.

LEARNING BIRD VOICES

How you learn bird calls and songs, and to what extent, is an individual matter. It will depend on the condition of your ears and on your ability to remember sounds, an ability that varies a lot from person to person. However, the more you can learn, the better a birder you'll be.

Birders use phonetic mnemonic devices for remembering many voices. Some species have been named for their songs, so they announce their identities; thus, the Killdeer calls *kill-dee, kill-dee,* and the Black-capped Chickadee sings *chickadee-dee-dee.* The songs of other species seem to translate naturally into musical phrases, so we easily hear an American Robin singing *cheerily cheer-up, cheerily cheer-up* or a Yellow Warbler singing *sweet, sweet, sweet, I'm so sweet.* Other representations are a bit more fanciful; the song of a Song Sparrow, at least in the East, has been represented as *sweet, sweet, WHAAAT-have-got-to-give-away?* The Barred Owl seems to call *who cooks for you, who cooks for you all?* a mnemonic that captures the rhythm of the call even more than its sound. Other mnemonics are almost entirely rhythmic, such as the Common Yellowthroat's *witchity-witchity-witchity-witch* or the White-throated Sparrow's *poor Sam Peabody, Peabody, Peabody,* which Canadians prefer to render *sweet, sweet Canada, Canada, Canada.*

Such mnemonics are valuable in writing field notes about an unknown singer, even with nonsense syllables such as *deedle, deedle, deedle; ooh-wah; pol-i-op;* or *p'witiop, p'witiop, p'witiop, pu* (to take some examples from my own field notes).

It would be a waste of both your time and mine for me to write much more about listening to birds' vocalizations. Instead, let yourself be guided by experts in learning about vocalizations, particularly by Richard Walton and Robert Lawson in their four *Birding by Ear* CD sets in the Peterson Field Guide Series. Walton and Lawson divide the species into groups that have similar calls and songs, which makes the process of learning much easier. Other CDs of bird vocalizations are available, arranged in standard checklist order; you may find Lang Elliott's *Stokes Field Guide to Bird Songs* valuable. Then let yourself be guided further by one of the masters of the field, Donald Kroodsma, through his book *The Singing Life of Birds*. The book contains a CD of bird voices to be used in conjunction with the text.

Studying and learning bird songs at home through such recordings is another aspect of the program I'm advocating in this book — preparing yourself before going into the field. Of course, one of the best places to learn songs is in the field. In both situations, an important general rule is to *look at the bird or a picture of the bird while listening to the song*. In the field, try to locate the singer. Spend some time watching it and making notes about its song; the combination of the visual and aural will help you learn a species' song. Some experienced birders have also emphasized the importance of connecting each song and singer with its habitat. The voices in the marsh, after all, are different from those in the field or forest.

To supplement the descriptors that Walton and Lawson use, it is helpful to have a vocabulary of nouns and adjectives for describing vocalizations, such as: buzzy, melodious, flowing, staccato, flutelike, fluting, thin, grating, trill, harsh, warbling, high-pitched, whistling, low-pitched. For instance, the songs of Clay-colored and Grasshopper Sparrows have been described as insectlike and buzzy, whereas Botteri's Sparrow is described (by Peterson) as "a constant tinkling or pitting, running to a dry trill" and Cassin's Sparrow has "a sweet high trill." One of the Blue Jay's common calls is certainly flutelike, and the *konk-la-ree* song of the Red-winged Blackbird has a liquid, somewhat fluting quality, with a trill or gurgle at the end. You will have your own opinion of each song, and describing it for yourself in some way will help you remember it.

A NOTE FOR THE HEARING-IMPAIRED

If you have experienced enough hearing loss to make it hard to hear some bird vocalizations — it is almost always the very high-pitched sounds that one misses — some help can now be found. Hearing aids are widely available, and if you go to ordinary sources you should test hearing aids against bird calls, perhaps by taking a CD of high-pitched calls along when you are testing devices and getting fitted. Some hearing aids with greater amplification of high-pitched tones are especially made for birders. Another approach is to use a device such as the SongFinder (www.nselec.com), which lowers the pitch of natural sounds into a range that people can hear more easily.

CHAPTER 10

When and Where
to Find Birds

Although you can see birds just about anywhere and at all times, some places and times are clearly better than others.

BIRDING RESOURCES AND GETTING CONNECTED

Unless you're a dedicated loner, you'll want to meet other birders and learn about birding organizations and other connections to birding information, such as where and when to go birding.

A good local connection is to a chapter of the National Audubon Society, which you can find through the usual community resources (the public library, city or county government, or your local newspaper), through the Audubon Society website at www.audubon.org, or by writing to National Audubon Society, 700 Broadway, New York, NY 10003. Your local chapter probably sponsors bird walks and more extensive birding trips, and these can be great ways to get to important birding areas and to meet new friends.

The American Birding Association (ABA) is the largest national organization devoted to birding, as well as to conservation and education. Contact ABA at www.aba.org or at 4945 N. 30th St., Suite 200, Colorado Springs, CO 80919.

Some of the best answers to the where-and-when question come, increasingly, from the many inexpensive, well-designed illustrated guidebooks to birding areas. There are now so many, for birding throughout North America and, indeed, all over the world, that I haven't even attempted to include them in the bibliography. Guides for your local area are available from your local bookstores, stores that carry bird feeders and other birding supplies, or from the ABA. Some of the best are in the extensive ABA Birdfinding Guide series, which now includes the most important American birding areas. With few exceptions, you can find guides to every state in the United States and to many specific localities. They have opened up birding adventures for everyone. You can fly to a distant city, rent a car, and drive to a promising region. The books, with excellent maps, will guide you to each spot and provide detailed instructions on where to go and what you may be able to see. In fact, they seem to make bird finding so easy that the greatest danger in using them may be disappointment at not seeing a bird that is supposed to be locatable somewhere.

In this electronic age, the opportunities for learning about birds and getting connected to birders are unlimited. Simply Googling *birding* or a related phrase will open wide the doors of ornithological authorities and birding enthusiasts. Here are some specific websites to check out.

National Audubon Society: www.audubon.org

The National Wildlife Federation: www.enature.com

Cornell University's All About Birds: www.birds.cornell.edu/AllAbout Birds/BirdGuide

Bird Links to the World: www.bsc-eoc.org/links/links.jsp

American Ornithologists' Union: www.aou.org

www.thebirdindex.com

www.birdingonthe.net

Interpretive Birding: www.ibirding.com

World Birding Center: www.worldbirdingcenter.org

www.birdcentral.net has natural history notes from the classic Bent series of life histories (see bibliography) and a variety of ornithological topics.

For bird sounds: www.naturesound.org

For those interested in owls: www.OwlPages.com

Devorah Bennu's website Birds in the News (www.scienceblogs.com/grrl scientist) provides weekly information about birds.

And the list goes on, seemingly endlessly.

Birders also stay in touch with one another through e-mail discussion groups (listservs) and through telephone hot lines, especially rare bird alerts (RBAs). One resource for this information is White and Lehman's *Guide to Birding Hotspots* (National Geographic Society), which describes important places to visit and has telephone numbers for RBAs and other resources. There is an RBA number for every state, plus some for local areas.

TYPES OF BIRDS BY SEASON

The maps in your field guides tell you about the range of each species, using pink for its breeding range and blue for its winter range, which produce a purple color where they overlap. Browse through these maps and see what they tell you. They not only alert you to the general presence or absence of a species at your location but also tell you whether you can expect to see the birds in breeding or winter plumage.

Birds are divided into categories on the basis of their yearly abundance and movements. The principal reason for changes in seasonal abundance is that many birds migrate, but birds also move around in random ways that can take them far from their usual ranges.

Many species of birds are *residents* that stay in one place all year. Some North American examples are Great Horned Owl, both Eastern and Western Screech-Owls, Hairy and Downy Woodpeckers, Common Raven, Tufted Titmouse, Black-capped Chickadee, White-breasted and Brown-headed Nuthatches, and Carolina Wren. You can expect to see them in their ranges at any time, and in more or less constant numbers all year. Many other species are residents throughout most of their ranges but shift southward in the winter so they are absent from their most northern reaches. Thus, many people living in the United States will experience them as residents, but for others they will be migrants. This may mean that the individuals you see during the winter breed farther north and have moved into your area temporarily, while those you have been seeing during the summer have moved southward.

Most North American birds are *migrants* that winter in the south, return to the north in the spring and spread out over North America to breed, and return to the south for the winter. Many species, especially small songbirds such as flycatchers and warblers, winter in the American tropics and make long journeys every spring and fall; the survival of many of these *neotropical migrants* is of real concern because many of their habitats are rapidly being destroyed in both North and South America. Other migrants, such as Greater Scaup, Glaucous Gull, Rough-legged Hawk, and Smith's Longspur, breed in the far north and come down into the United States during the winter. Some species migrate up and down the mountains. In Washington and Oregon, for instance, Varied Thrushes breed in the mountains and come down to the lower elevations during the winter, as do the three species of Rosy-finches that breed in the highest mountain peaks.

Northern irruptives don't engage in a regular movement southward in the winter, but an occasional irruption (not *eruption*) brings them south in unusual numbers. Well-known irruptive species include Red and White-winged Crossbills; Common and Hoary Redpolls; Evening Grosbeaks; and Great Gray, Snowy, and Boreal Owls. These southward irruptions occur when high-level northern populations experience shortages of food. So we may see unusual numbers of finches if the crops of seeds produced by the northern conifers have fallen short, or owls may come south in unusual numbers if there are shortages of the lemmings and voles they feed on. These irruptions may occur in a regular cyclical manner that people can predict, so that when a species is likely to irrupt, observers can be alerted. Northern Shrikes, for instance, have a peak about every four years. If you are linked into a good birding network, you'll hear about them as soon as other birders start to see them.

Other species appear here and there, now and then, irregularly and unpredictably. *Vagrants* are birds that have strayed from their migration routes; occasionally a warbler or vireo shows up far from its normal route, generating great excitement among birders. *Casual* birds are those that don't appear annually in an area but show up in small numbers unpredictably, so over a period of years there is a pattern to their occurrence. For instance, Northern Wheatears breed in various places in northern Canada and Alaska, but during the winter they are casual in southern Canada and the northeastern United States. *Accidentals* are birds that have occurred only a few times in odd places; just about any bird could be an accidental.

Birders get a special kick out of chasing these rarities; a report of an accidental sticking around for a while can get many birders into their cars or onto planes, traveling hundreds or thousands of miles to see it.

Pelagics are birds of the open seas that rarely appear near land. Many of these birds are migrants, but sometimes on a cycle opposite to those of land birds. Many oceanic birds breed in the Southern Hemisphere, where it is summer during our northern winter. After breeding, they disperse to other oceans, so we see them as nonbreeding birds during our summer. Look at the maps of Greater and Sooty Shearwaters (maps E13 and 14), for instance, or Wilson's Storm-Petrel (map E17).

Given these patterns of migration and abundance, start by becoming acquainted with the patterns of birds where you live, at least the most common birds. Your local Audubon Society or some other local bird club very likely has checklists that give some of this information for your area. This information is especially easy to obtain for a region that has one of the local guidebooks I referred to earlier. These guides now commonly include a pictorial representation of the abundance of each species, like the one on p. 97 from the ABA Birdfinding Guide *A Birder's Guide to Eastern Massachusetts.*

The width of each line shows the relative abundance of a species at each time and region. This is especially valuable for a beginner or for a visitor to an area, because it is a guide to reasonable expectations. As you struggle with the fundamentals of identification, it helps to know which species you are most likely to see. Of course, this is a balancing act; there is always the chance of an accidental showing up, of a bird lingering in the fall long after its compatriots have migrated south or arriving in the spring long before it is "supposed" to.

These considerations of rarities aside, you'll benefit from studying the abun-

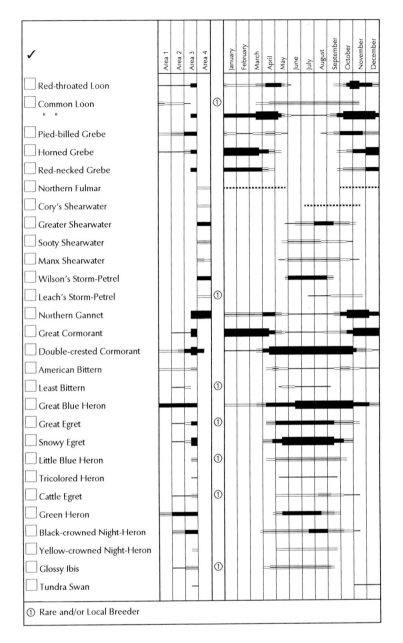

✓	Area 1	Area 2	Area 3	Area 4	January	February	March	April	May	June	July	August	September	October	November	December
☐ Red-throated Loon																
☐ Common Loon					①											
" "																
☐ Pied-billed Grebe																
☐ Horned Grebe																
☐ Red-necked Grebe																
☐ Northern Fulmar																
☐ Cory's Shearwater																
☐ Greater Shearwater																
☐ Sooty Shearwater																
☐ Manx Shearwater																
☐ Wilson's Storm-Petrel																
☐ Leach's Storm-Petrel					①											
☐ Northern Gannet																
☐ Great Cormorant																
☐ Double-crested Cormorant																
☐ American Bittern																
☐ Least Bittern					①											
☐ Great Blue Heron																
☐ Great Egret					①											
☐ Snowy Egret					①											
☐ Little Blue Heron					①											
☐ Tricolored Heron																
☐ Cattle Egret					①											
☐ Green Heron																
☐ Black-crowned Night-Heron																
☐ Yellow-crowned Night-Heron																
☐ Glossy Ibis					①											
☐ Tundra Swan																

① Rare and/or Local Breeder

dance charts and making a list or calendar of your own. Just when should you expect to see the various thrushes or warblers or blackbirds in your region? When will the great hordes of shorebirds come through your area in the spring, and when will they begin to trickle back through in the late summer? Although you will inevitably encounter a few birds at unexpected times and places, you can make your entrance into birding a lot easier by writing out some general patterns. Other birders in your area probably already have good records of migration times, and as you widen your network of birding acquaintances, you can get access to these, but you'll also benefit from doing some of the work yourself.

PLACES FOR BIRDING

One obvious place to watch birds is your home. Birding at home is easy; you don't have to dress specially (or at all!), and you can see a great deal in warmth and comfort while you think of all the birders out in the extremes of broiling deserts or freezing winter winds. This is especially attractive for disabled people for whom walking is a burden and for those who lack their own transportation. (If transportation is the main reason for staying home, however, be assured that birders, on the whole, form a most generous community, and if you connect with a local birding group you will certainly make friends who will be happy to give you a ride.) Furthermore, it's easy to attract birds to your home with feeders and attractive plantings. Many people like to keep a home list or a feeder list of all the species they have seen in their yards or at their feeders.

The second most obvious place to go birding is your neighborhood, especially if the homes are well landscaped with trees and other plants, and most especially if there is a small park in the area. I suggested earlier that to get started in birding you should find a good spot where you can go regularly, and that might be right in your own neighborhood. A local area with a lot of mixed vegetation can produce a surprisingly long list of species, and your neighborhood might be an oasis in the midst of a more severe urban area, which will attract many nesting birds. By taking the same route day after day, you may discover some nesters and follow their progress in nest building and raising their broods. The area may also be a green patch that attracts birds passing through a large city during migration. A little urban park could be all yours to enjoy early in the morning.

Beyond your immediate neighborhood, the opportunities for birding expand enormously. First, consider larger parklands in your region. County and state parks can provide excellent adventures for the naturalist, even if some of the land is devoted to playgrounds, campsites, and cabins. These parks often feature nature trails, and because of the growing interest in birding, they often have lists of the local birds at the trailhead, marked by their abundance in each season. Developed natural history trails make walking relatively easy and take you to interesting spots, such as a good observation point at the side of a marsh.

There are many wildlife refuges across the United States, situated to protect precisely the birds and other wildlife that you want to see. Many are operated by private organizations such as the National Audubon Society and The Nature Conservancy. Others are governmental, operated by the U.S. Fish and Wildlife Service or other agencies. These can be among the most exciting places in the world to go birding. You are lucky if you live within easy driving distance of one. As with parks, these refuges provide developed trails, literature on the local wildlife, and, often, tours through the area by bus or tram.

CHAPTER 11

Birding Techniques and Etiquette

SIMPLE RULES FOR SUCCESS IN BIRDING

Dress in Subdued Colors

People who want to get close to the natural world have a wardrobe of dull-colored clothes that help them blend into that world. White is particularly bad, as it scares certain birds. Browns, tans, and khakis are good, though few birders go to the extreme of wearing military camouflage uniforms.

Listen; Speak Little, and Quietly

Use your ears to locate birds. Directional hearing is important in helping you find a bird's location. Experts locate nine out of ten birds in this way. While you are birding, your conversation ought to be very muted and confined to essentials, such as pointing out where you see a bird or discussing what you're seeing and trying to identify the bird. The time for socializing is in the cars, vans, or buses on the way there and back, not in the field.

Walk Slowly and Quietly

Birding is different from taking a brisk walk for exercise. Move slowly, turning this way and that, scanning the sky, constantly searching your surroundings, while your ears are attuned to the slightest sound that might be made by a bird or another animal. Tread softly. Every sound of a twig snapping alerts and flushes wild animals, so walk heel to toe, contacting the ground as gently as possible. Also, don't let your arms make a repetitive swooshing noise by sweeping over a bulky jacket, and avoid corduroy pants, which make a soft rasping sound as you walk.

Don't Loom Suddenly into an Open Space

Before entering a new space — such as a clearing in the woods or a wetland at the edge of a forest — stop and move into it slowly, looking carefully before you're actually in it. You should expect to encounter different birds in this new habitat, and you can startle them with your sudden appearance.

Don't Always Be on the Move

Stop sometimes. Wait. Watch and listen. One of the best birding strategies is to stay in a good place largely hidden by the surrounding brush, sit quietly, and let the birds come to you. One of my colleagues, who is a master of this technique and teaches it to students, says, "Don't just do something — sit there!" He tells about a group of children who were being taught to do this and were sitting quietly in a circle and waiting. One child happened to be holding a stick, and a bird came and sat on the stick for a while right in front of her eyes. When they did the exercise again the next day, every child was holding a stick.

"Go West, Young Man!"

The early morning is the best time for observing land birds, especially during breeding season. They're up and active, feeding, singing, making a delightful racket — the dawn chorus — and are generally easy to find. So happy birders tend to be early birders, up well before dawn and out in the field. Then take the advice popularized by Horace Greeley in 1851: try to go west, with the morning sun at your back, so the light falls on the birds in front of you rather than in your eyes.

Use Actions Appropriate to the Setting

You're a big, threatening animal, and birds will get nervous when you appear. That's bad for both you and the birds. It's bad for you because you want the birds to be calm and go about their usual activities while you watch. It's bad for the birds because they're distracted from their important business of feeding and breeding, and one of the rules is that their well-being is more important than your desire to see them.

In many locations you are likely to flush a bird when you encounter it. When this happens, freeze. Wait. In the best case, the bird will fly a short distance and perch, so you can watch it. Or if it flies into the bushes, it will probably stick around the area, and if you'll just be patient for a few minutes, it may come back to where you can observe it.

You have binoculars for watching birds move around in a normal manner from a moderate distance. But you might want to get a little closer. Distance closing is tricky. Do it slowly, gently, carefully. Try not to move directly toward the bird but obliquely, at an angle. You should appear to the bird as if you don't really care about it. Take a few steps and then stop and observe. Take a few more steps and stop. In trying to get closer you might agitate the bird; it might start calling, jumping from branch to branch, and generally looking as if you're infringing on its territory. In that case, back off. The bird's welfare is more important than yours.

The wisest behaviors around large birds are often different from those around small birds. One admonition about speaking is "When around ducks, talk like sparrows; when around sparrows, talk like ducks." This follows from the (apparent) fact that birds' ears are most attuned to the sounds made by others like them, so small birds, used to making and hearing high-pitched sounds, are less likely to notice low-pitched sounds. In general, actions that might scare small birds away may have much less effect on large birds. When observing small birds or birds that seem skittish, try to keep your binoculars high, near your eyes, so you don't have to make sudden wild movements that may be alarming. Quick movements around any birds are ill-advised, of course, but they are most agitating to little birds.

Watch for Movement

Movement often reveals a bird's location. But a swinging branch is more likely to be the spot that a bird has just left than a spot where a bird has just landed. Also, understand the "scissors effect." Look at a pair of scissors opening and closing; the point where they meet — the point where they actually cut — moves along the blades. Now put yourself in the woods surrounded by many tree trunks and branches poised at different angles; as you move — or as the wind moves them — these trees and branches will cross one another in your line of sight, and the points where they cross, just like the scissors blades, will appear to be moving things out there in the woods. Try not to be unduly distracted by them.

By the way, as you bring your binoculars to bear on distant objects that you hope are birds, you are going to find yourself looking at leaf-birds, lump-birds, clump-birds, funny-looking-knobs-on-branches-birds, and other things that simply are not birds. Look at them, because they might be birds, but once it is clear that they aren't, don't waste your time on them. Just get used to being fooled in this way.

Call Birds in with Good Judgment

Birds are attracted to the sounds made by others of their species as well as sounds made by other species. Many birds, for instance, are attracted to the calls of small owls, which they mob in an effort to scare off these predators. So you may be able to attract many birds by playing recordings of them or by using a method called pishing. At first, this sounds like a terrible thing to do out in public, but it's not what you think! Birders commonly attract birds by pishing, which means making little hissing and squeaking sounds in various ways. Some people make a squeaking sound by sucking noisily on the back of a hand; others squeak by sucking air with the tongue or lips against the teeth, or they may use a repeated high-pitched whisper such as, *psss, psss, psss* or *pssh, pssh, pssh.* Everyone has a favorite method. The National Audubon Society sells a little device that can be rotated to make a squeak. Pishing is most effective when you stop in a secluded spot, settle down and don't move, and then start to make your sound. Be patient. You may soon find several curious birds moving in quite close.

Just why pishing works is not clear. Some have hypothesized that the noise is like the calls of a young bird in distress calling its parents. The birds may be responding out of simple curiosity, though you know what curiosity did to the cat and what it might do to a bird. Furthermore, pishing doesn't universally work. Some species are attracted easily; others aren't. American birders commonly use this trick, but some people traveling abroad have reported that birders in other countries don't know the method and that the birds in other places don't respond like North American birds. No one knows why.

Although relatively benign, pishing and playing recordings are a bit controversial. By calling birds in these ways, you may be disturbing their nesting and feeding activities, so ethics dictate that these methods be used judiciously. In some places, such as national wildlife refuges, it is simply illegal to play recordings of bird calls and songs.

Don't Get in Others' Sightlines

While birding with other people, be aware of where they are looking and avoid stepping into their lines of sight. In the excitement of looking for a new bird, it's easy to shift your position unconsciously and not realize that you have just moved in front of someone's scope.

Be Specific in Helping Others Locate Birds

One of the chief advantages of birding in a group is that many eyes together can spot birds that a single pair of eyes might miss. So a part of your obligation in a group is to keep watching and call people's attention to anything they might not have seen. If a bird has just zipped over everyone's head and has gone on to parts unknown, it isn't very useful to say anything about it unless you were able to identify it. But if it zipped by and then landed in a bush, where it may still be lurking, tell someone, because the group might be able to spot it. Call attention to birds overhead as quickly as possible, because they may be visible to everyone for only a few seconds. Identify them as much as you can: "Ducks coming in from the south, over the tree line, now over the tall tower . . ." or better yet, "Looks like Pintails heading east to west, just over those birches now." But you're still being helpful if you can say only "Oh, look at those big birds right over-head!" because someone else may be able to identify them.

Beginners tend to just point in the direction of a bird they see in a tree or bush nearby and say, "It's right there!" Right where, pray tell? Learn to be as specific as possible: "On the large birch about twenty feet out, right side, about ten feet up, moving out on a branch pointing up at about forty-five degrees." That may seem to be asking a lot, but notice what useful information you can learn to provide: (a) a specific kind of tree, so it's good to become a general naturalist and learn to identify the principal plants found in your area or the area you're visiting; (b) a distance from you and from the ground, so it's good to learn to judge such things. But if this seems too complicated, there are at least two other simple but useful methods. One is to carry a small mirror, so on any reasonably sunny day you can direct a beam of light toward the bird — never directly *at it,* for goodness' sake, but in a small circle *around* its location. (And please do *not* use the little laser pointers; the bright spot they produce, though easily visible, could blind a bird, and who knows what creature in the bush you might blind without knowing?) A second useful method, especially with a bush, is to treat it as if it were a clock face and use the o'clock method of specifying where the bird is. "Small bird at about ten o'clock in that cottonwood, now moving toward twelve o'clock."

Go Birding Alone

Beginners can certainly benefit from going on field trips organized by local Audubon Societies or other bird clubs, and magazines devoted to birding or nature activities in general carry many ads for organized trips to just about every interesting birding spot on earth. If your budget permits, you'll probably want to take advantage of some of these trips. For starters, though, I recommend that you find places nearby where you can easily go alone or with a friend. There are advantages and disadvantages to both approaches. You can learn a lot from more experienced birders who can take you to good places, demonstrate good birding technique, and help you identify new birds. On the other hand, one of the underlying principles of this book is that people learn only — or at least learn best — what they do for themselves, and the effort to learn birding as outlined here will make you stronger and more confident. There is also great satisfaction to be had from the sense of accomplishment you get by doing it yourself.

USING BINOCULARS

Initial Adjustments

If you've bought a new pair of binoculars (see appendix 2), you need to adjust them properly. Even if you've been using your binoculars for some time, it may help you to do the initial exercise as if they are new, because you may not be using them to best advantage.

First, be sure your binoculars are set for the proper interpupillary distance — the distance between the centers of your eyes — so that you can see a single round field with a clear image. Next, make sure you have the proper *eye relief*, which means having your eyes at the proper distance from the eyepieces so that you can look through the binoculars comfortably. You generally achieve this by adjusting the eyecups that are on every good pair of binoculars. If you don't wear glasses, you'll probably want to keep the eyecups extended so they surround your eyes somewhat and shade them from extraneous light. If you do wear glasses, you'll need to adjust the eyecups to get your eyes as close to the oculars as possible — the closer they are, the larger your field of vision will be — while achieving proper eye relief. This may require turning the eyecups down completely.

Finally, compensate for the difference between your eyes with the *diopter adjustment*, a rotating ring on the right eyepiece. (Some expensive new binoculars have the diopter adjustment built in in a different way.) Find a comfortable spot where you can focus on an object 30 to 60 feet away, ideally a neatly lettered sign on which you can see sharp edges. Rest your arms on a steady support, or at least be able to hold the binoculars steady. (See below for advice about steadying your binoculars.) With your right eye closed or covered comfortably, use the center focus knob to get the clearest, sharpest image of the object with your left eye. Then close or cover your left eye and look with the right; *being careful not to move the focus knob,* rotate the right-eye adjustment until this image is sharp and clear. Repeat this procedure once or twice to be sure you have the best images with each eye separately, then you should be able to see a sharply focused image with both eyes, with none of the strange, not-quite-right quality of image that occurs with ill-adjusted binoculars.

A line or dot on the right eyepiece will be aligned with some point on a scale, generally a scale marked + in one direction and – in the other. Note that point exactly. On good binoculars, the diopter adjustment will stay where you set it, but it might be displaced a little as you use your binoculars. If your diopter adjustment tends to get out of place and you don't mind how your binoculars look, you can keep it in place with a wide rubber band.

Stability

Though how to hold your binoculars might seem obvious, it can be difficult to keep them steady and avoid fatigue. You've surely bought binoculars of a weight you can handle so you can hold them in position reasonably well, but seriously consider an exercise program to strengthen your arms, because they really can get tired as you hold up your binoculars for extended periods. Fatigue will make it hard to hold your glasses steady, but even when not fatigued, our arms and hands naturally make little involuntary movements, which you want to minimize while watching birds.

As a wearer of eyeglasses, I get a lot of stability just from resting the binoculars against my glasses; moderate pressure on your glasses shouldn't force them against your nose uncomfortably. But if you find this uncomfortable or if you don't wear glasses, experiment with getting stability by using either your eyebrows or your cheekbones. Try grasping your binoculars closer to the eyepieces than you usually do, but still far enough forward so you can easily manipulate the focus knob. Experiment 1 is to raise your index fingers slightly and rest them against your eyebrows to see if you can achieve a comfortable, stable position. Experiment 2 is to extend your thumbs somewhat and rest them against your cheekbones to see if that is a comfortable, stable position. Try fooling around with these positions for a while; this is a highly individual matter, and you have to balance comfort and stability with achieving the proper eye relief and being able to focus the binoculars quickly and easily.

Keeping Them Clean

Dirty optics are probably most responsible for robbing you of good vision. The lenses, especially the eyepieces, need regular cleaning. Yet you can damage your fine lenses by cleaning them carelessly. The junk that settles on the lenses is abrasive, and casually rubbing it off can scratch the glass. First, remove the worst dirt by blowing with a little puffing instrument sold for cleaning camera lenses, or with canned air under pressure. Second, remove remaining obvious dirt by *lightly brushing* with a fine, clean brush. Finally, carefully remove the remaining film with one of the fine lens cleaners sold for eyeglasses or other optical lenses. Your binoculars should have a lens cap on the straps that slips down over the oculars whenever you're not using your glasses and falls aside as you raise them. Get in the habit of checking this, especially when it's raining, to be sure your eyepieces stay as clean and dry as possible.

Finding Birds and Looking

Now you're ready to use your clean, well-adjusted binoculars that you can hold steady. But wait. It's easy to get into the habit of clamping your bins to your eyes as soon as something appears that you're intent on seeing, but that isn't always the best practice. With your eyes alone, you can see an enormous amount and take great pleasure in the seeing, and you are best able to judge two things: the bird's size and its family. You can compare its size to other objects around it, and you can see the general patterns of shape and behavior that are so critical for determining what kind of bird it is. Furthermore, your eyes alone command a wide visual field; binoculars cut that field to a very small area. When a bird appears in that wide field, it's natural to want to get your binoculars on it right away, but this may be hard to do, especially if the bird is moving around. So you can spoil the chance to enjoy a great view of the bird with the naked eye as you fuss around trying to get your glasses on it; by the time you get them focused on the last place the bird paused, it may have taken off. The pleasure of seeing a bird unaided will often be more rewarding than the high-tech method.

Nevertheless, most bird watching requires binoculars, and the greatest problem people have is getting them on the bird quickly and accurately. Beginners tend to let their eyes fall to their binoculars as they are raising them. Instead, *keep looking at the bird and raise your binoculars into your line of sight.*

As you raise your binoculars, it helps to be able to pick out landmarks that identify the right spot. The area will look different at 7 or 8 power than it does with the unaided eye, and it is useful to be thinking something like *Right side of trunk, branch drooping at thirty-degree angle,* or *Patch of yellow leaves,* or *Long twig hanging straight down.* If you immediately see this landmark through the binoculars, you'll know you're in the right place, and you can — ideally — locate the bird relative to it. Yet the bird may have moved while you've been trying to get your binoculars on it. If you don't see the bird within a couple of seconds, drop the binoculars slightly below your eyes and look again with your unaided eyes. You can probably locate the bird in a new place, and with the binoculars already so close to your eyes, you have a better chance of finding it in the binocular field when you look again. (This is why a wide field of vision is valuable.) While trying to get a good look at a bird, you are likely to observe for a short time, then drop your binoculars slightly to find the bird again, and continue to alternate between looking with and without binoculars. Remember that in general it's useful to keep your binoculars near your eyes so you don't have to make sudden wild movements with your whole arms, movements that are likely to alarm birds.

Another technique for using binoculars depends on the existence of *focal planes* (see drawing on p. 107). An optical instrument such as a telescope or binocular is focused on objects in a focal plane at a certain distance, and it creates a sharp image of those objects in another focal plane at the lens of the eye. Turning the focus knob of the binoculars shifts the focal plane to objects that are closer or farther away. This focal plane has a certain depth, so everything within that narrow range is essentially in focus and everything outside it appears blurred. You can use this fact to pick out a bird on a branch somewhere inside a fairly dense bush by shifting the focal plane to the bird's position; the bird will be in focus, but branches and leaves around it will be fuzzy — don't let that bother you, and focus your attention on the bird. Where the foliage is extremely dense, as in the tropics, you can focus your binoculars on a plane within the tangle — perhaps shifting the plane back and forth just a little — to bypass the brush that otherwise would obstruct your view.

Exercises in Using Binoculars

Now for practice. Remember the rule: Keep your eyes on the target and move the binoculars *into the line of sight.* Resist any temptation to look down at the binoculars. To practice this, walk around some area such as your yard or a large room in your house and use your binoculars to look at things. Keep your eyeballs steadily on the desired point and move the glasses into your line of sight, again and again. As you practice this, notice whether you can generally hit the right spot or if you tend to first hit a spot consistently in one direction from the target — say, just a little below it. If you do, add a correction to your initial motion. Then practice some more, making the proper corrections until you can hit the target consistently.

At the same time, you have to learn to focus quickly and correctly. Few things in birding are more frustrating than seeing a fuzzy image of a bird and then losing the bird before you can focus your glasses. Out in the field, it helps to have a good idea at all times of roughly where the binoculars are focused. Then be absolutely sure which direction to turn the focus knob to get nearer or farther vision, and practice focusing on objects at different distances until you become really good at it. From time to time, you'll undoubtedly start to turn the knob the wrong way, but you should correct quickly.

Now go out and start watching birds. A bird feeder near your house could be a good place to practice at first; you can switch between looking at birds right on the feeder and those waiting on nearby trees or other perches at varying distances. Then branch out and start looking at birds at all distances, including flying birds, and work on developing your skill.

PART II

Some Problematic Groups

CHAPTER 12

Females

Birders naturally love brilliantly colored birds such as tanagers and grosbeaks, but the birds that sport incredibly gorgeous plumages are often males whose female counterparts are very dull, obscure, and easy to ignore. Yet the road to expertise requires paying some attention to these females.

Species whose males and females look different are *sexually dimorphic* (*di-* = two; *morph* = form). For some species, it's not much of a stretch to recognize and identify both sexes. For instance, as you're becoming acquainted with American Kestrels, it's easy to see that a bird with blue-gray wings is a male and one lacking the blue-gray color is a female. You can differentiate male and female Belted Kingfishers just by seeing if a bird has a rusty breast-band.

EXERCISE 12-1. The sexes of many woodpeckers differ only in the presence or absence of a red patch. Show where this patch is located for each of these species or how the female differs from the male.

Pileated: _____

Northern Flicker: _____

Downy: _____

Hairy: _____

Red-bellied: _____

Yellow-bellied Sapsucker: _____

Red-naped Sapsucker: _____

Nuttall's and Ladder-backed: _____

The females that are most likely to be confusing are certain passerines. Sometimes we encounter flocks with some puzzlingly colored birds, which turn out to be females that we can identify by their association with easily identified males, as explained below. Sometimes, however, we encounter a bewildering female alone. This poses an identification problem, which I'll divide into three types: the yellow-bird problem, the streaked-bird problem, and the little-brown-job problem.

We can often narrow down a problem by asking what I will call the General Location Question (GLQ): "Where am I and what is the date?" We'll see how important it can be to think about your location and the time of year. A puzzling bird on the midwestern prairies in the summer is almost surely different from a puzzler in Minneapolis or Boston in the winter.

The Yellow-Bird Problem

The yellow-bird problem can be divided into three stages of eliminating possibilities.

STAGE 1.

EXERCISE 12-2. Both males and females of two passerine families discussed in chapter 6 generally have a lot of yellow and olive in their plumage. What are these families?

_____ and _____

So a yellowish bird may be one of these. Remember that we can distinguish one family from the other by the birds' behavior and by their bills. Describe these differences:

EXERCISE 12-3.

Behavior: _____

_____

Bills: _____

_____

The members of both families have relatively small, thin bills adapted for eating insects, and if you're looking at a puzzling bird with such a bill, it's likely to be a warbler or vireo. Now look closely at some of the warblers in the field guides: E261, 265, 267, or W289, 291, 295. The combination of their patches of yellow mixed with other colors — especially black, gray, and white — marks them well as warblers, and the females of these species are generally pale versions of the males. So with a little practice and field experience, you won't confuse them with other families of birds, and you'll learn to identify these species.

STAGE 2. In contrast to the warblers we've just looked at, look at the very different warblers on E269, 271, 273, 275, or W299, 301, 305. Here are birds with olive above and yellow below, and some of the vireos have the same general pattern: E257, 259, or W285, 287. The problem is that there are similar birds that aren't warblers or vireos. To make the situation clearer, let's lay out some of these images and compare them.

Philadelphia Vireo female

Yellow-throated Vireo female

Nashville Warbler female

Wilson's Warbler female

Connecticut Warbler female

Hooded Warbler female

Scarlet Tanager female

Summer Tanager female

Baltimore Oriole female

Orchard Oriole female

Now you can see that several species of passerines, especially the females of the species, have upperparts in the range of yellow-green to olive to brown and underparts with a lot of yellow. But juxtaposing these images also reveals the keys to solving the problem. We've already seen that you can separate warblers from vireos on the basis of their bills and their behavior, among other aspects of their gestalts. Now let's take account of the tanagers and orioles. First, remember that orioles are members of one of the families of passerines introduced in chapter 6.

EXERCISE 12-4. What family do orioles belong to, and what are the distinctive features of the family?

_____

_____

EXERCISE 12-5. Next, you may want to review one of our first lessons about field marks (Exercise 2-10, p. 23). What are the three principal features that distinguish tanagers and orioles?

_____

EXERCISE 12-6. With these features in mind, study the drawings of tanagers and orioles above, as well as the similar vireos and warblers. Then explain how you can use the features discussed here to distinguish the females of these four groups.

_____

_____

_____

_____

_____

_____

_____

Some helpful hints for answering this question are in the Answers section in appendix 1. The purpose of this analysis is to narrow the identification to one family. Then if you determine that the bird you're studying is an oriole or a tanager, the next step is to turn to the plates of these groups in the field guides and narrow the identification to one species.

STAGE 3. Suppose a puzzling yellowish passerine has the conical seed-cracking bill of a sparrow or finch instead of the bill of a warbler, vireo, tanager, or oriole. Then what could it be? One answer is on E291 or W345. Evening Grosbeaks and the three species of goldfinches commonly move about in flocks, and though the females of these species are rather washed-out versions of the males, you can identify these females by their associations with their easily identified males. You are most likely to see Evening Grosbeaks when a little flock appears at a feeder. Female American Goldfinches are also pale and lack the black caps of males, but goldfinches, too, commonly move about in little flocks and nest in colonies, so it is easy to identify some of them as females. The same is true of the Lesser and Lawrence's Goldfinches, with their more restricted ranges. When you find a flock of these birds, take the opportunity to study them and become more familiar with both sexes, especially the females. Notice how green Lesser Goldfinch females are.

Suppose, however, your yellowish bird with a finchlike bill isn't in a flock and doesn't fit the description of an Evening Grosbeak or one of the goldfinches. One possibility is a female Painted Bunting, which is very green — Peterson points out that no other small finch is all green. Now it becomes important to ask yourself the GLQ. Look at the range of the Painted Bunting, map E423. If you aren't in that range at the right time of year, you can eliminate Painted Buntings. But if you find yourself in the ranges of the next two maps, E424 and 425, and especially if you're in a grassland, you must consider Dickcissels and Bobolinks (E319, 313; W347, 309). Female Dickcissels don't show much yellow, so they may be more of a streaked-bird problem than a yellow-bird problem, and you may know them best by their associations with males, the "little meadowlark" of the grasslands. Female Bobolinks are more of a buffy yellow, and they, too, will be associated with males.

The Streaked-Bird Problem

The females of some species with spectacularly colored males are camouflaged with nondescript brownish streaking. Sometimes this is hardly a problem. In a colony of Red-winged Blackbirds in a marsh, while the brilliantly adorned males are displaying their epaulets and calling, their well-camouflaged mates may be moving unobtrusively through the reeds but their identities will be obvious. Take the opportunity to observe the females closely, paying attention to their icterid bills, so you will recognize them if you see them unescorted.

Similarly, you will encounter flocks of Pine Siskins in the winter, especially at feeders; the males are distinguished from the females by yellow in the wings and tail, which is often hardly visible. So the nondescript little streaked birds may be of either sex.

This leaves a few species whose streaked females could give you fits: the Rose-breasted Grosbeak (E287; W337) and the three *Carpodacus* finches: House, Purple, and Cassin's (E293; W343). The problem of separating them from one another and from similarly plumaged sparrows edges toward advanced birding, as described in Kenn Kaufman's *Advanced Birding* field guide. In this situation, I think you should just try to observe the birds' bills closely and distinguish the obviously huge bill of the grosbeak — *gros* means "large," after all — from the smaller bills of the finches.

The GLQ can also help to sort out these birds. Consider your location and consult the range maps as well as whatever information you can glean about times of abundance, as discussed in chapter 10. So if you answered the question by saying, "I'm in New York and it's July," a puzzling streaked bird might be a female Rose-breasted Grosbeak or a female *Carpodacus* finch, either a House Finch or Purple Finch. If, however, you were in Quebec at that time, you would probably eliminate the House Finch from serious consideration, while in the mountain West you would add Cassin's Finch.

Another streaked-bird problem can arise during breeding season on the American prairies, where the stark black-and-white plumage of male Lark Buntings identifies them immediately. The female Lark Buntings have nondescript streaked plumage, and because their bills are rather large, you might confuse them with some female finches. But if you say to yourself, "Hey, I'm in the middle of Montana and it's July and there are male Lark Buntings flying all around me," you might reach the logical conclusion: "Those are probably female Lark Buntings." (See E318; W347.) You will strengthen that conclusion if you notice that these birds have whitish wing patches.

The Little-Brown-Job Problem

This distinguished category includes females of the Blue Grosbeak, Indigo and Lazuli Buntings, House Sparrow, Brown-headed Cowbird, and perhaps the Bobolink. Identifying some of them also verges on advanced birding, though it is a situation that Kaufman doesn't handle, and it is tied up with the general issue of learning the sparrows, chapter 16.

This problem is partially solved by asking yourself the GLQ. Bobolinks breed only in a band across the middle of the continent during the spring and summer, then they migrate to South America. Blue Grosbeaks and the buntings breed over broader ranges and also migrate south of the border for the winter. The cowbirds, however, are much more broadly distributed, and they remain in North America. House Sparrows are largely urban and social, so you are likely to observe the females in the presence of males.

To supplement the place-and-time consideration, again notice the bill of an unknown bird in this category: large on the grosbeak, medium-sized and somewhat curved on the cowbird, small and finchlike on the buntings. It will also help to see that female Brown-headed Cowbirds are quite gray and have the somewhat more elongated bodies of blackbirds, rather than the more compact bodies of sparrows. The female buntings, however, are about as nondescript as a little bird can be. Don't feel bad if one of them remains a mystery, but we discuss them in more detail in chapter 16.

CHAPTER 13

Diurnal Raptors (Hawks)

Watching and identifying hawks can be a joy and a thrill, and birders generally count it an especially good day when they find more than a few of the most common hawks. Some observers devote their birding lives to identifying hawks at the spots where they pour through by the thousands during fall migration — one of the truly spectacular sights of birding. My personal view is that hawks can be so exciting that as a novice you can gain enormous pleasure from them even if you can't identify every bird.

One Peterson Field Guide is devoted to hawks, and if you catch the bug, several other excellent books will help you pursue the group to the limits of observation. Some of them will introduce you to a more holistic, intuitive way of identifying hawks by means of subtle clues of shape and movement — by their *jizz*. But beginners, to use a cliché, must learn to walk before they can run, and you must first become well acquainted with hawks by learning their field marks.

As with other large groups of birds, the critical first step is recognizing the principal categories. Although hawks and falcons are distinct groups, I'll use the general term *hawk* here casually and include the New World vultures in this discussion, even though they are carrion eaters rather than raptors and are probably related to storks. (Notice that both vultures and storks have bald heads.)

Peterson points out that even from a long distance we can separate out three members of this group in flight.

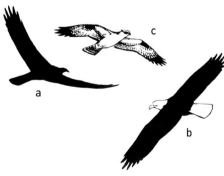

Over most of the continent we commonly see Turkey Vultures (a) hunting on a warm day, gliding with the dihedral in their wings. Eagles (b) soar on flat wings, and Ospreys (c) soar with a kink in their wings, generally while hunting over water.

Most other hawks belong to three categories that can be separated in flight by their overall shapes. Hawks commonly soar by ordinary flapping or by riding rising columns of warm air called thermals, which can carry them to great heights with little expenditure of their own energy. Once aloft, a hawk can circle an area and hunt or move off, as in migration, by setting its wings in a different position and gliding for long distances. So their shapes change somewhat in soaring or gliding.

BUTEOS: Broad, rounded wings and a broad tail, especially when soaring. They commonly soar high in the sky, wheeling and turning as they ride the thermals upward and search for food.

full soar   glide

ACCIPITERS: Rather short, broad, rounded wings and long, narrow tails. They commonly live in woodlands, where they hunt small birds, and they fly with a few flaps followed by sailing.

full soar

glide

FALCONS: Pointed wings, narrow tails.

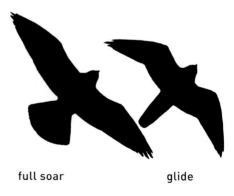

full soar   glide

Northern Harriers, members of a different group, are easily identified and are good candidates for the common, easy birds category. We almost always see harriers gliding low over fields as they hunt, with a strong dihedral in their wings and an obvious white rump patch. Overhead, they also present a distinctive shape: long rounded wings and a long tail.

When perched, the three main types of hawks look like this:

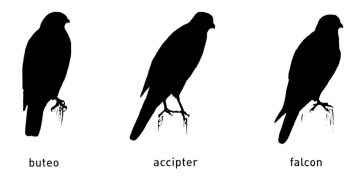

| buteo | accipter | falcon |

Perched buteos are most distinctive because of their heavy, robust shape and rather short tails. The other two have quite long tails, and accipiters have smaller heads than the others.

Buteos

Over the continent as a whole, the buteo you're most likely to encounter is the Red-tailed Hawk. In the East, you are also likely to see Broad-winged and Red-shouldered Hawks; in the West, Swainson's and Ferruginous. In the middle of the continent you'll encounter all five. So concentrate at first on these five species, starting with those most common in your area. The situation is complicated by the fact that four species of buteos have a *dark morph* in addition to the more common *light morph; morph,* which simply means "form," indicates a genetic difference, just as humans have different colors of eyes, skin, and hair. We are all *Homo sapiens* in spite of these differences, and both light- and dark-morph Ferruginous Hawks are *Buteo regalis.* The genetic difference makes life both interesting and difficult for birders, and my advice for novices is to *ignore the dark morphs* for a while and just record them in your notes as dark buteos.

Let's first deal with *adult buteos, both perched and in flight* — ignore the immatures for now, as well as the dark morphs.

EXERCISE 13-1. For birding in the East, diagnose perched Red-tails, Broad-wings, and Red-Shouldered Hawks (E101, 103).

_____

_____

_____

_____

_____

_____

_____

_____

EXERCISE 13-2. For birding in the West, diagnose perched Red-tails, Swainson's, and Ferruginous Hawks (W175, 177).

_____

_____

_____

_____

_____

_____

_____

_____

EXERCISE 13-3. For buteos in flight in the East, use E107 to diagnose Red-tails, Broad-wings, and Red-Shouldered Hawks.

_____

_____

_____

_____

_____

_____

EXERCISE 13-4. For buteos in flight in the West, use W193, 195, to diagnose Red-tails, Swainson's, and Ferruginous Hawks.

_____

_____

_____

_____

_____

_____

We encounter the other buteos in restricted ranges: Short-tailed in Florida, White-tailed in Texas, Harris's and others in the Southwest. Rough-legged Hawks come down from the far north in the fall and winter, to southern Canada and most of the United States except the extreme south. In the northern part of this winter range, from late autumn through early spring, the only buteos present may be Rough-legged and Red-tailed. You'll know Rough-legged Hawks by a white uppertail patch, easily visible from above when a bird is gliding, and by the combination of a black belly-band and black wrist (carpal) patches at the bend of the wings (E107; W193).

EXERCISE 13-5. Both Ospreys and Rough-legged Hawks have black wrist patches and black bands on the tails. How can you distinguish one from the other (E107, 115; W189, 191)?

_____

_____

_____

Accipiters

Our three species of accipiters are easily recognized as members of this group by their distinctive shape in flight and their flight pattern of a few flaps and a sail. But distinguishing them from one another presents some challenges. In fact, experts are often puzzled and may disagree with one another; as a beginner, you will be doing well just to call a bird accurately as an accipiter and leave it at that. One problem is that we frequently encounter immature birds, which look very much alike (E99; W173). Accipiters live by hunting small birds, and this is a tough way to make a living, as their prey species are as well adapted for escape as the predators are for attack. (I have a vivid memory of a Cooper's Hawk with a screaming Steller's Jay in its talons. The hawk landed on the ground only a few feet away; the jay somehow wriggled out of the hawk's claws and, still screaming, ran into the bushes to safety.) So many individuals simply don't get enough nutrition to grow to adulthood.

If, however, you want to pursue the question of identifying species, there are a few general guidelines. You can't rely on size. Since females of each species are larger than males, there is a continuum of sizes, female Sharpies being similar to male Cooper's, and so on. Most observers depend on the difference between the rounded tail of the Cooper's and the square tail of the Sharpie. ("Sharpie, sharp tail corners.") This mark is not 100 percent reliable, but you'll be right much more often than wrong by using it. Experienced observers also rely strongly on the way a Sharpie's small head barely projects in front of its wings in flight, whereas a Cooper's head sticks out clearly. So this is a situation in which careful reading of Peterson's analysis combined with gradually developing field experience will be your most reliable road to success.

Falcons

These birds stand out because of their pointed wings. Kestrels are some of the common, easy birds — note their unique rufous plumage. (A falcon perched on a wire is almost certainly a Kestrel, and a hovering falcon is _always_ a Kestrel.)

Gyrfalcons are rare visitors from the North during the winter, and Aplomado Falcons are restricted to a few sites in Texas and the Southwest, where they are recovering from near extinction. So your principal problem here is to recognize Merlins and Peregrines and, on the western prairies, Prairie Falcons.

Perched birds — or those that you can see well enough in flight — are most easily distinguished by their facial patterns, with emphasis on the patches or streaks commonly called mustaches (though they remind me more of sideburns).

EXERCISE 13-6. How do you distinguish Merlins from Peregrines if you can see their heads well (E117; W187)?

_____

_____

But we commonly see these falcons in flight — for instance, when one of them hangs around an area frequented by migrating shorebirds and quickly flies in for an attack.

EXERCISE 13-7. How can you distinguish Merlins from Peregrines in flight (E117; W187)?

_____

_____

Vultures

Leaving aside California Condors, which are engaged in their own dramatic fight for survival, there are only two North American vultures, and they are easy to distinguish in flight (E93; W183). Black Vultures have short fan-shaped tails and prominent white "windows" in their wings. It will also help to study their distribution maps.

Kites

Kites form another group of hawks (E94, 95), but they vary so much that characterizing them as a group isn't really useful. Swallow-tailed Kites (E97) are so unusual that you could never confuse them with another species. Snail Kites and Hook-billed Kites are restricted specialties of Florida and Texas, respectively, and you have to go to specific sites at certain times of day to find them. Both species feed primarily on snails. To find Snail Kites, follow the directions in Pranty's guide to finding birds in Florida, and make local inquiries about the best spots; arrive at a likely place in the late afternoon, shortly before sunset, and wait. To find Hook-billed Kites, go to one of the Rio Grande Valley refuges such as Bentsen or Santa Ana early in the morning and inquire about the best places to see them. As the air warms up and thermals start to rise, the kites will come out of the woods for a short time, when you can spot them, and then they retire to the woods to feed.

EXERCISE 13-8. Mississippi and White-tailed (formerly called Black-shoul-dered) Kites need some analysis, and even they are quite restricted in their ranges. Study the plates of kites and explain how to tell one from the other (E97; W171).

_____

_____

_____

QUIZ

1. A bird with this shape flies up from a wood-land. What is it?

_____

2. What general type of bird is this? Do you see some specific features that identify the species?

_____

_____

_____

3. You see a bird with this form overhead, and you immediately know that you're seeing a

_____

4. What field mark do you see here? What general kind of bird is it? What species?

_____

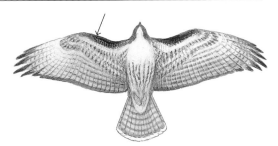

5. You might see this bird overhead anywhere on the continent. What general type of bird is it? The arrow points to a prominent field mark that immediately identifies it to species; what is that mark, and what is the species?

_____

_____

6. What features do you see on this perched bird that identify it to a category?

_____

7. What type of hawk is this? Do you see a field mark that probably identifies the species?

_____

_____

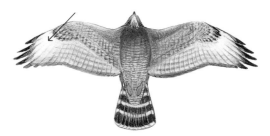

8. You may see this bird throughout much of the East. What is the feature to which the arrow points? What other field marks can you see, and what is the species?

_____

_____

9. What do you see here?

_____

10. This small bird has just taken off from an over-head wire. What is it and how do you know?

_____

_____

11. This rather small bird is common in the East. What field marks do you see, and what is the species?

_____

_____

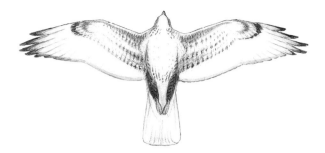

12. You see this bird overhead on the Great Plains. What field marks do you see, and what is it?

_____

_____

13. Can you see two field marks on this bird? What species is it?

_____

_____

14. Two of the buteos are known in part by their tail markings. What species are these?

_____

_____

15. Driving along the freeway, you see a robust perched hawk with a light breast and a streaky band across its belly. What is it?

_____

16. Name two species that glide with a dihedral in their wings.

_____

_____

CHAPTER 14

Shorebirds

It's a beautiful spring day at the height of the shorebird migration, so let's go down to a beach or mud flat and see what we can find. Wow! Look at them all! Thousands of little birds spread out across the sand and mud. Occasionally a little flock rises from the mud and starts to fly back and forth along the water, hundreds of birds moving as if with a single mind, turning with balletic synchrony, flashing their wings in harmony like some gigantic semaphore, and then settling down on the mud to feed again. It's one of the great sights of bird watching.

And, as Peterson noted, one of the most puzzling for the beginner. But it doesn't have to be. It will be easier to tackle shorebirds in general if you're already acquainted with Killdeer — and ideally with Spotted Sandpipers, too — so you recognize the typical shorebird form. Then we'll sort them all out bird by bird, little by little, primarily by learning *genera* of shorebirds. Incidentally, we'll ignore species that are rare accidentals from Asia or Europe.

First, two important points about the biology of these birds.

Distribution and migration. Examine the range maps of shorebirds (maps E137–76; W113–53). Notice that the vast majority of them breed in the far north or in the midwestern prairies. We will take special notice of those prairie species later because North Americans can see them easily on their breeding grounds; most shorebirds are easily accessible to many of us only during migration or during the winter, as several species winter on or near the coasts. We usually see massive numbers of shorebirds moving northward in April and early May; upon reaching their far north breeding grounds, they reproduce quickly during the short northern summer, and by late in the summer they start heading south, often in much more somber basic plumages, making them generally harder to identify. So the most rewarding time to be out watching shorebirds is during that brief time of spring migration.

Feeding. Thumb through the shorebird plates, paying particular attention to the birds' bills. (And see E138 and W128.) The remarkable range of bill sizes makes sense if we consider that shorebirds feed primarily by probing their bills into soft sand and mud to find minute animals.

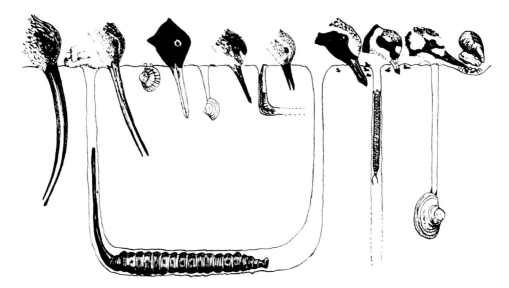

From left to right: Whimbrel, Hudsonian Godwit, Black Oystercatcher, Dunlin, Red Knot, Black-bellied Plover, Semipalmated Plover, Ruddy Turnstone.

The bills of various lengths are clearly used for feeding at different depths, and the shorebirds demonstrate better than any other group of birds the ecological strategy of *niche differentiation*. The birds divide the resources — the small animals they feed on — by adopting different feeding strategies. In this way they avoid direct competition with one another so several species can coexist. Some of the long-billed birds that frequent the prairies also use their bills as probes for insects aboveground, among the grasses and flowers.

An Easy Lesson in Sorting Shorebirds

Now let's look at a typical mud flat scene during the spring. We come to it from the upland side, so the water is most distant. *Without using your binoculars,* look at the area of bare mud and sand; it's probably covered with small birds that seem to be moving around like mad, but if you pick out individual birds and watch them for a few seconds, you'll see that they are actually moving in *two distinct patterns.* Some of them really are in almost frenzied, constant motion, pecking at the mud at machine-gun speed; these are the *sandpipers.*

But others stand still for a few seconds, perhaps peck at some little animal on the mud, run a few paces, stand still again, then run ahead a few paces, and so on; these are the *plovers*.

So by means of this simple observation, we've separated two major groups of shorebirds. Now notice also (you may have to use your binoculars for this) that sandpipers have longer necks than plovers, and sandpipers' bills are generally thinner and longer than the short, fat bills of plovers.

plover   sandpiper

We'll return to these birds in a moment.

As we are separating the sandpipers and plovers by their general behavior, you may find little shorebirds with an outstanding black-and-white head pattern and rufous backs rushing about and probing under rocks and shells. These are the aptly named Ruddy Turnstones (E150; W142), which really do hunt by turning over stones and other objects to find food under them. Though not the most common birds on the mud flat, they are easy to spot.

Now look beyond the mud flat to where the mud and sand meet the shallow water. Some slightly larger birds with much longer bills are probably there, many standing in the water with their bills pointed downward and their heads going up and down like sewing machines. These are *dowitchers*. In the same general region, or in slightly deeper water, you may see

taller shorebirds with longer bills — godwits, curlews, and similar birds, which we'll return to later.

So by merely looking closely, hardly even using our binoculars, we've separated most of the shorebirds into a few categories that we can focus on, starting with the sandpipers.

Sandpipers

Most sandpipers have thin bills of short to medium length, and they generally feed on the surface of the mud or just beneath it. During the spring, you should be able to pick out many that have distinct *black belly patches* and moderately long, droopy-tipped bills: the Dunlin (E153; W141). Since it is so easy to spot the Dunlin, study them to become familiar with their bills and the general form of their bodies. Dunlin will be our prime example of *calidridines*, the members of the genus *Calidris (ka-LID-ris):* short-legged, compact sandpipers with short necks and moderate to short bills. (We'll meet some taller calidridines later, but for now we're pretending they don't exist.) You may also see some slightly larger, fatter sandpipers on the beach with distinctively *robin-breast red-orange underparts* and somewhat heavier bills; these are Red Knots (E151; W139).

You can easily pick out Dunlin and Red Knots. But most of the little sandpipers on the mud flat are probably some similar calidridines called "peep," primarily Semipalmated, Least, and Western Sandpipers (E159; W149).

EXERCISE 14-1. In their breeding plumage, how can you distinguish the peep as a group from Dunlin?

_____

_____

_____

It's easy to identify peep as a group: rather plain little birds — emphasis on *little* — with brownish upperparts and very light, somewhat streaked underparts. Trying to distinguish one species from the others, however, gets close to advanced birding, or at least intermediate-level birding. You probably don't want to venture into that realm yet. If you aren't content with just calling them peep at this point, here are a few things to notice about them:

Least Sandpipers stand out to a degree because they are relatively brownish;
   Western because they are distinctly rufous on the back and head.
Least also stand out because of their very thin bills.

Westerns stand out even more because their longer, heavier bills droop at the
tip. (This drooping is most pronounced in females, and there is enough individual variation so not all Westerns show it clearly.)
Least have yellowish or greenish legs, in contrast to the black legs of the others.

Your location will also help you to a degree — ask the GLQ. For instance, on
the East Coast during the spring, the vast majority of peep will be Semipalmated, while on the West Coast during the spring, about 90 percent of the peep
will be Western. The other two American species that are called peep — Baird's
and White-rumped Sandpipers (E157; W147) — migrate primarily through the
middle of the continent in the spring and then return more broadly over the
continent in the fall, largely in the East along the Atlantic Coast. Ultimately, such
geographic points won't help you identify an individual with certainty, but as
you work toward such expertise, they may help you gain confidence and reduce
the number of possibilities you must consider.

Plovers: *Charadrius*

Let's turn to the plovers on the mud flat and beach. The more familiar you have
become with Killdeer, the easier this will be. Killdeer are husky shorebirds with
uniformly brown backs and *two* breast-bands standing out on starkly white
breasts. On this basis, you should be able to pick out Semipalmated Plovers,
which look like miniature Killdeer with only a *single* breast-band. These two
species can be our models for the genus *Charadrius* (*kah-RAD-ree-us;* E135;
W125).

EXERCISE 14-2. What are the characteristics of a *Charadrius* plover?

_____

_____

_____

_____

Aside from the ubiquitous Killdeer, Semipalmated Plovers are the *Charadrius*
you're most likely to see over most of the United States during migration or in
the winter; they are virtually the only *Charadrius* you'll see in migration along
the West Coast. In most of eastern North America, the other *Charadrius* you may
see sometimes is the Piping Plover, a declining and endangered species associated with sandy and cobble-and-shell beaches.

EXERCISE 14-3. What field mark best distinguishes a Piping Plover from a Semipalmated Plover?

_____

_____

Piping Plovers have variable breast-bands, sometimes partial and sometimes full. As a species, Piping Plovers are in serious trouble; relatively few breeding pairs are left because of human interference with their habitats along the Atlantic Coast beaches and rivers and the lakeshores of the northern prairies. They winter on the southern Atlantic and Gulf coasts. Because of their endangered status, we must all be particularly careful about approaching them, especially during breeding season.

The southern Atlantic and Gulf coasts also host Wilson's Plovers, an uncommon species you may well ignore until you become more familiar with other _Charadrius_ species. Identifying it requires making some subtle distinctions that Peterson notes, in the heaviness of the bill and the width of the breast-band.

Finally, you will have to contend with Snowy Plovers on some restricted breeding areas: a patch in the southern prairies and an irregular patch mostly in Nevada and Utah. They winter along the Gulf and Pacific coasts.

EXERCISE 14-4. Snowy Plovers are similar to Piping Plovers; look at E135 or W125 and explain how to tell one from the other.

_____

_____

Plovers: _Pluvialis_

Their startlingly black undersides immediately identify plovers of the genus _Pluvialis (ploo-vee-AIL-iss)_, at least during the spring. These are two species of American Golden-Plovers — which were not even distinguished until 1993 — and the Black-bellied Plover. (The European Golden-Plover is a rare vagrant.)

EXERCISE 14-5. By studying plates E133 or W123, determine the most obvious field mark that distinguishes the breeding Black-bellied Plover from the Golden-Plovers.

_____

_____

EXERCISE 14-6. Look at the range map W114. Where do you expect to see the two North American species of Golden-Plovers?

_____

_____

_____

EXERCISE 14-7. It helps to know where you're most likely to see these birds, but study the plate again (W123) to find a field mark that distinguishes the Pacific Golden-Plover from the American.

_____

_____

_____

Dowitchers

Returning to our view of the mud flat, we note the dowitchers feeding mostly at the water's edge. The two species — Long-billed and Short-billed — cannot be separated by the lengths of their bills.

Females have longer bills than males, and there is considerable overlap in lengths. Many observers distinguish them by their calls, the high-pitched _keek_ of the Long-billed contrasting with the _tu-tu-tu_ of the Short-billed. They can also be distinguished by their plumage, but this requires close observation of some details, and it is best left as an aspect of advanced birding.

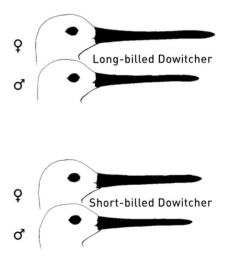

On the Sandy Ocean Beaches

Many of the migrating shorebirds that gravitate to mud flats also appear on the sandy beaches along the oceans, where we may find little flocks of the various plovers and sandpipers, perhaps with some of the godwits and curlews discussed below. These ocean beaches are the particular habitat of some pale little calidridines that look like peep but chase the waves on the beach rather than moving about randomly. As a wave moves up the sand, they run up with it, and as it recedes, they follow it back toward the water. These are the Sanderlings (E153; W141). Enjoy their antics. Get to know them so you can identify them easily. They continue wave chasing in their winter habitats along the coasts, and in winter (basic) plumage they are extremely light in color, another point to notice.

EXERCISE 14-8. In their winter plumages, Piping Plovers (E135; W125) are very similar to Sanderlings (E153; W141), but recalling one of the first lessons about watching shorebirds, you can tell one from the other even without binoculars. How?

_____

_____

_____

Rocky Coasts and Some Specialists

Some of the most interesting shorebirds are specialists of rocky coastlines, including human-made jetties and breakwaters. A calidridine that breeds in the high Arctic and Greenland, the Purple Sandpiper (E151), is most likely to appear in such a habitat in the winter along the Northeast coast, or perhaps in the Great Lakes area. Notice how similar it is to our paradigm calidridine, the Dunlin; it has a similarly drooping bill, but with its very short neck it presents a rather plain, dumpy aspect.

Rocky coasts in the West host an unusual group of shorebirds during the nonbreeding season, the "rockpipers" (W142–43). They make for fascinating viewing during the winter, providing a challenge good for training the eye to see details. Especially with a good spotting scope, you can observe these birds perched on the rocks, and when provoked into a brief flight from rock to rock by the waves breaking around them, they display distinctive black-and-white patterns that aid their identification.

EXERCISE 14-9. Study W143, with special attention to the small drawings that show the birds in flight, and explain how to distinguish Wandering Tattlers, Rock Sandpipers, Surfbirds, and Black Turnstones from one another.

_____

_____

_____

_____

_____

_____

_____

With good protection against the biting wind and blowing surf, you can have a fine time watching these interesting little birds.

The Tall Shorebirds

The curlews, godwits, and other large shorebirds are spectacular, with their impressive bills. What could they possibly be confused with? One answer is "Waders such as herons, egrets, and ibises" — that is, members of the order Ciconiiformes. So begin by comparing the large shorebirds (E143; W131) to some of the large herons and egrets (E46–53; W110–17), especially the ibises, whose bills may look like the bills of curlews until you examine them closely.

EXERCISE 14-10. Make some notes here about the differences between ciconiiforms and tall shorebirds:

FEATURE	CICONIIFORMS	TALL SHOREBIRDS
Bills		
Necks		
Plumage		

The best overall distinction is probably in the sizes of their bills, as the heavy, spearlike bills of ciconiiforms contrast sharply with the much thinner bills of shorebirds. Even the ibises, which beginners might confuse with curlews, have bills that are heavy all the way to the tip, whereas the curved bills of curlews become very thin at their ends. Ibises have distinctive plumages, too, but note the caveat that immature ibises are brown, somewhat like curlews. Habitat can also be an important clue. Ciconiiforms mostly frequent marshes and shallow lakes and streams; shorebirds are more likely to be on mud flats and beaches or in dry habitats such as meadows and fields, where they commonly breed.

The Greater and Lesser Yellowlegs are common tall shorebirds in sloughs and along the shorelines of lakes and rivers. The yellow of their legs is so obvious that with a little experience you'll immediately say, "Yellowlegs!" Their behavior helps to distinguish one species from the other, as Greaters are very active feeders that are likely to be carousing around, chasing minnows and calling attention to themselves, while Lessers feed much more quietly. Also, notice if the bird's bill is about the same length as its head (Lesser) or if the bill is clearly longer than the head and commonly somewhat upturned (Greater).

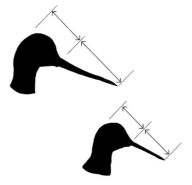

This a good time to take note of a sandpiper related to the Yellowlegs, the Solitary Sandpiper. Approaching an isolated woodland pond or the banks of a quiet stream, you may encounter a moderately tall, dark sandpiper that flies away (flashing a black-and-white tail pattern) unless you're careful to be unobtrusive. The Solitary Sandpiper is well named. Virtually all the other shorebirds are highly gregarious; you may find them flocked together by the thousands. The Solitary is a maverick, a bird that really wants to be alone.

You may often encounter a bird that looks like a Greater Yellowlegs, though a bit stockier and without yellow legs; puzzling, because it seems to have hardly any outstanding markings. Then suddenly it will fly and reveal a spectacular black-and-white pattern on its wings. This is a Willet (E149; W135). After you've seen a few Willets, you'll learn to recognize them quickly by their plainness and their heavy bills.

The other tall shorebirds are either curlews, with decurved bills, or godwits, with upturned (or nearly straight) bills.

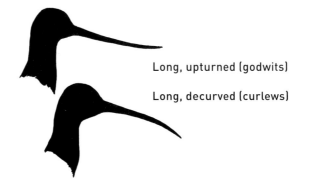

Long, upturned (godwits)

Long, decurved (curlews)

First, the curlews. Ignoring the occasional accidental from Eurasia, we have only two curlews in North America: Long-billed Curlews and Whimbrels (E143; W131). Eskimo Curlews are probably extinct; if you think you see one, check your enthusiasm, make the best possible field notes and drawings, and then get an experienced birder to come and take a look. Your first encounter with Long-billed Curlews may elicit awe and some disbelief that any bird could really be carrying around such a schnoz. The bills of female Long-billed Curlews are so different from those of Whimbrels that it is hard to confuse one species with the other (or with any other species); the bills of male curlews are shorter than those of females and may approach the size of a Whimbrel's bill, but you can overcome any confusion posed by their similarity with your answer to the following exercise.

EXERCISE 14-11. Find a good field mark other than the bills that distinguishes Whimbrels from Long-billed Curlews.

On the way to their far-northerly breeding grounds, Whimbrels migrate along both coasts (where you are likely to see them) and then head inland to their breeding grounds, where they feed on small animals, including worms and insects. In migration, they sometimes join the shorebirds that feed in the mud along the water, but you may also find them inland feeding in dry fields. Long-billed Curlews also feed largely on crustaceans and worms, which they extract from holes and crevices with their incredible bills.

Finally, the godwits. We also have only two species, aside from accidentals. Hudsonian Godwits migrate north through the prairies, where they might present some problems of identification with the Marbled Godwits, but in the fall the entire population of Hudsonians gathers around James Bay and Hudson Bay and then flies south rapidly to South America. If you carefully examine flocks of godwits and are very lucky, you may have the additional problem, or joy, of identifying the rare Eurasian accidentals: the Bar-tailed and Black-tailed Godwits.

EXERCISE 14-12. Following the field marks in the guides (E143; W131), determine how you can distinguish breeding-plumaged Hudsonian from Marbled Godwits (a) when they are standing and (b) when they are flying.

_____

_____

_____

_____

Four Large Unmistakables

Four large shorebirds are so distinctive and interesting that you can hardly misidentify them. The North American coasts are home to two big silly-looking birds with bright red bills: the American and Black Oystercatchers. The American has black-and-white plumage; the Black entirely black. Both are strictly coastal, and the Black favors rocky coasts, so you may see it in the same habitats as the smaller rockpipers.

The Black-necked Stilt and American Avocet are members of the same family (Recurvirostridae), even though they look nothing alike. As Kenn Kaufman remarks in his book _Lives of North American Birds,_ "Everything about the Black-necked Stilt seems delicate — from its incredibly thin stilt-legs to its slim wings and its needlelike bill." When combined with its unique black-and-white plumage, these delicate features make it easy to spot in a shallow-water habitat (see map E145 or W120 for its range). Its relative the Avocet also has an incredibly thin bill, clearly upcurved, and slightly different black-and-white plumage with a gorgeous cinnamon brown head and neck.

On the Prairies

Though most shorebirds breed in the far north, the North American prairies are the summer homes of several species and the major migration route of others. These wonderful places to visit on a spring or summer day can present some challenges for birders. The prairie birds demonstrate that the term _shorebird_ is sometimes a misnomer, because several species, nicknamed "grasspipers," frequent grasslands and dry fields, where they feed on insects and other invertebrates rather than probing in the mud or water. First, examine the range maps of these species.

> Upland Sandpiper (maps E152; W128)
> Mountain Plover (map W118)
> Long-billed Curlew (maps E154; W130)
> Marbled Godwit (maps E156; W132)
> Willet (maps E150; W125)

These species all breed in the Great Plains and parts of the western United States. The range map of the Upland Sandpiper shows it occurring in the Northeast, but it is declining in much of that part of its range, and its population is stable only through the Great Plains. Out on the prairies in the spring and summer, you probably will not have much trouble identifying the larger birds. Now look at the Upland Sandpiper (E155; W145), a bird of moderate size with a few field marks, which often perches on posts and typically lands with its wings spread. With its long neck and medium-sized bill, it stands out in this habitat. For a time in the middle of summer, Uplands may be the only bird of this approximate size and shape on the prairies, but during spring and fall migration, the situation becomes more difficult. These plates with the Upland Sandpiper also feature the Buff-breasted and Stilt Sandpipers. These three species give an impression of tallness, uprightness. (The Stilt Sandpiper is actually a calidridine, so different from others of its genus.) We have to consider them together during migration, as they all migrate through the prairies in both spring and fall. Stilt Sandpipers gravitate toward shallow water and mud, the other two toward grassy areas.

EXERCISE 14-13. What field marks distinguish Upland, Buff-breasted, and Stilt Sandpipers?

_____

_____

_____

_____

_____

_____

Three other species largely associated with the prairies (also calidridines) remain to be analyzed: White-rumped, Baird's, and Pectoral Sandpipers (E157; W147). All three migrate north through the prairies. They return to the south along the same route, except that White-rumped Sandpipers move off to the Atlantic Coast in the fall, and Pectorals migrate south over much of the United States.

EXERCISE 14-14. What field marks can be used to distinguish White-rumped Sandpiper (E157; W147)?

_____

_____

EXERCISE 14-15. What field marks can be used to distinguish Baird's Sandpiper (E157; W147)?

_____

_____

EXERCISE 14-16. What field marks can be used to distinguish Pectoral Sandpiper (E157; W147)?

_____

_____

Phalaropes

You probably won't encounter the Red-necked and Red Phalaropes much, as they breed in the Arctic and migrate primarily at sea, where they also winter. They're most often seen on a pelagic trip several miles offshore, but we occasionally find them on ponds in coastal regions. Wilson's Phalarope, however, breeds on the western and midwestern prairies, including the southern Canadian prairies, and winters in South America, so you are more likely to see it in migration along the coasts. Prepare to see phalaropes by noticing their delicate, thin bills (though the Red Phalarope's bill is more like those of other shorebirds) and the gray-and-white patterns of plumage on fall migrants. Notice also that these shorebirds commonly swim, and they feed by spinning like tops, apparently to stir up small animals and bring them to the surface.

CHAPTER 15

Gulls

Gulls are a universal nemesis of birders. Looking at gulls in the field, your first impression may be that there are a lot of clean-cut white-and-gray gulls that all look alike and a lot of brownish, dark gray gulls that all look alike. Then it turns out that the brownish, dark gray gulls are immature white-and-gray gulls, and at that point you may be ready to throw the whole lot of them into your mental wastebasket and forget all about them. And, of course, you can. I'll suggest that at first you should try only to go a moderate distance in identifying gulls, because so much of gull identification really is an aspect of more advanced birding. Gull experts recognize species by means of very subtle clues, such as whether a bird's face looks "fierce" or not. Audubon Societies offer identification classes specifically about gulls and specifically about the immature gulls, and these are classes for people who are already well experienced in other aspects of birding.

The first point to learn about gulls is to not call them "seagulls." Few species are really found at sea; they frequent ocean shores and inland bodies of water. And one way to get yourself labeled as a hick birder to be shunned is to be heard saying "seagull." So don't say it.

The second point is that there is a good reason why it is so hard to identify some gulls: Several species of gulls aren't well sorted out. We saw in chapter 2 that populations may be in an intermediate stage of speciation, only partially separated from others, so the whole group of populations is best called a *superspecies* and its constituents are *semispecies*. Speciation has occurred in a circumpolar *Larus* complex as populations have spread out east and west to leave a ring of races, including Iceland, Thayer's, California, and several Eurasian gulls; they hybridize with one another in varying degrees where they meet, and yet the ends of the chain — Lesser Black-backed Gulls *(Larus fuscus)* and Herring Gulls *(L. argentatus)* — come together again in Europe and act like well-defined species that do not hybridize. At some places in the Arctic, however, they are a taxonomic mess; it is difficult to cleanly label each bird as one type or another, so birds keep showing up that are terribly puzzling to even the best field observers. In spite of all this, however, gulls redeem themselves as subjects of study because they typically sit still for a long time and often allow observers to get quite close, so we can see important field marks such as the colors of their eyes, bills, and legs. (This is the result of a treaty with the gulls worked out in 1969 by the American Ornithologists' Union.)

Telling Gulls from Terns

How to distinguish gulls from terns is best learned through experience in the field. On the whole, terns are more delicate than gulls, and they fly with a subtle grace that gulls lack. Almost all terns have forked tails; almost all gulls have fan-shaped tails. Terns typically fly with their bills turned down toward the water, and they often hover for a few seconds and then dive into the water. Gulls seldom dive. With a little experience watching these birds, you won't have any trouble with the distinction.

Getting Acquainted with Gulls

Step 1. Ignore the immatures. Seriously, even though you'll notice the many brownish birds associating with the clean-cut birds of white, gray, and black, happiness lies in just writing them off as immatures and not trying to identify them at all. Yet.

Step 2. Learn how to *see* gulls. (I forbade the word *seagull* so you wouldn't make up silly verses about how to see seagulls.) To really get to know gulls well, you will have to learn to see details of their *bills, legs,* and *eyes,* but that's for later. At first, pay attention to two larger features of a gull: the *mantle* — the broad expanse of back and wings that is visible from above — and the *wingtips.* Using the plates of adult gulls (E177, 179, 181; W91, 93, 95, 97), answer the following questions.

EXERCISE 15-1. The mantles of gulls obviously range from pure white through shades of gray to black. Discriminating shades of gray can be tricky, especially in paintings or photos, but name some species with mantles of these shades:

Nearly pure white: _____

Light, silvery gray, almost white: _____

Light to medium gray: _____

Dark gray: _____

Black: _____

EXERCISE 15-2. Describe features of the wingtips of some species that set them off from the rest of the mantle on a flying bird.

_____

_____

_____

_____

    As you become acquainted with gulls, you will become sensitive to the shades of gray and will see that even a bird whose mantle looks almost pure white, such as a Glaucous Gull, is really a very light gray with wingtips described as "frosty" — pure white. The point about wingtips is that those of some species are essentially the same as the rest of the mantle, but other species have tips of a contrasting color, so it's important to take notice of them. Look at the white-black-white in the tips of a Franklin's Gull or the large wedge of white on a Bonaparte's or Black-headed Gull — more than just the tip, really. Look at the black tips of Herring, Ring-billed, and California Gulls, in contrast to the medium-gray mantles. Looking more closely at these black wingtips, you'll see white spots, called _mirrors,_ within the black. Notice, incidentally, that gulls rarely have a more complex pattern on the mantle; the Sabine's Gull with its gray, white, and black is a real exception.

    Step 3. Notice that the gulls are divisible into two classes: large, 24–32 inches long; and small, 11–17 inches long. (Later I'm going to lump two species of intermediate size in with the large ones for learning purposes.) Several of the smaller birds have black hoods in breeding season, and though they lose this hood in their basic plumage, they retain distinctive patterns and spots of gray. Let's concentrate first on these small hooded gulls.

Laughing Gulls

    These are the common small gulls of the Gulf of Mexico and halfway up the Atlantic Coast. Even nonbirders seem to know them as they wheel overhead crying _ha-ha-ha-ha-ha._ If you live anywhere along this coastline, get to know these little guys, and notice that their mantles are dark, even darker near the tips.

Franklin's Gulls

    These are the common small gulls of the northern United States and southern Canadian prairies, a species to know if you live in this region. Elsewhere in the West, we may encounter them during migration, but for the most part they winter out in the Pacific.

EXERCISE 15-3. What field mark identifies an adult breeding Franklin's Gull in flight?

_____

Bonaparte's Gulls

These little gulls breed from Alaska through western and central Canada, so many people living in that region will know them well in their alternate plumage, but most of us encounter them during migration or during the winter along the Atlantic, Gulf, and Pacific coasts. Along the Atlantic and Gulf coasts, this may create a problem for residents already acquainted with Laughing Gulls, but look carefully at the winter Bonaparte's and Laughing Gulls (E181).

EXERCISE 15-4. How can you separate basic-plumage Bonaparte's and Laughing Gulls by the patterns of their head plumages?

_____

_____

This analysis should simplify life with small gulls. The plates of small hooded gulls show three other species of similar gulls, but you will probably encounter Sabine's only out at sea on a pelagic birding trip. The Black-headed and Little Gulls are Eurasian species (for the most part) that appear infrequently along the Atlantic Coast and perhaps on the Great Lakes. You'll have to pay attention to them eventually if you are birding in the Northeast, but that will be a refinement in your growing knowledge of these birds.

Two other small gulls — Ivory and Ross's — appear so rarely south of their Arctic homes that you can ignore them for now. If one of them appears, you'll hear about it through a birding network. Some people take a special trip to Churchill, Manitoba, to see Ross's Gulls. You could, too.

The Large Gulls

To understand the larger gulls, we'll first mix in our two medium-sized gulls — the Mew and Ring-billed — with them. Though they are distinctly smaller than the others, I think it is asking too much of a beginning observer to see this difference right off. Instead, strive to see the difference as you gain experience in watching gulls; after a while it will become easy, and size will become one of the first features you use to separate out these two species.

EXERCISE 15-5. To begin winnowing this bunch down, study the range of the Great Black-backed Gull (map E194), an important species to know if you are anywhere in the Northeast. These common birds are so large and have such outstanding plumage that you can hardly mistake them for anything else, except possibly for Lesser Black-backed Gulls, which appear rarely within this range. A Lesser is clearly smaller and will stand out in a flock of Great Black-backed Gulls for this reason alone, and Peterson notes another significant feature that distinguishes the two: What is it?

After singling out the blackest species, look at the other end of the spectrum, the whitest species: Glaucous and Iceland Gulls (E177; W95). They appear rarely but regularly in the Great Lakes, down the Atlantic Coast, and (Glaucous only) Pacific Coast. These, too, are species that you will probably see only through a birding-network alert, and I think it requires a lot of experience of seeing other gulls to note how extremely light the gray of their mantles is. So for now set these species aside, too.

The Lesser Black-backed and Iceland Gulls are the most distinctive members of that complicated Arctic superspecies. One other member, Thayer's Gull, is another rare winter visitor, which I suggest you ignore for now until you're ready to deal with their subtleties and complexities. That leaves only two species of this complex that need concern us much in North America: Herring and California Gulls. The Herring Gull is one of the most common North American gulls, ranging throughout the East and Midwest (map E189). California Gulls are common in the West, and although they breed in the northern Great Plains, you will rarely see them elsewhere in the East.

EXERCISE 15-6. Find at least two characteristics that separate California Gulls from other similar gulls.

Throughout eastern and central North America, the most common issue is distinguishing Herring Gulls from Ring-billed Gulls. Both have medium-gray mantles with black wingtips. Ignoring their difference in overall size for now, look closely at the bills of gulls of this general type, a task that will help improve your ability to see gulls well.

EXERCISE 15-7. Describe an important difference between Herring and Ring-billed Gulls.

_____

_____

The situation is different in the West. Along the Pacific Coast, most of the large gulls you see will be Glaucous-winged or Western. They are easily distinguished, on the whole, by their mantle colors (W91, 95), except that they hybridize in Washington and British Columbia, making birds with the silver-gray mantle of Glaucous-winged plus very dark wingtips. You can learn to see these hybrids in a flock of gulls, or you may choose to ignore them for now until you become more experienced.

The Yellow-footed Gull, formerly considered a subspecies of the Western, breeds in the Gulf of California and then comes up to the Salton Sea area in the summer. Leaving it aside, the medium to large gulls we see commonly in the West are the California, Mew, Ring-billed, and — at least in winter — Herring. Along the East Coast, Mew Gulls — the European Common Gulls — are rare visitors from Europe; a North American race of the Mew Gull breeds in western Canada and Alaska, so for westerners it is a common winter bird farther south.

EXERCISE 15-8. We've seen that the bills of some species have distinctive field marks, but now let's consider all four of them and take into account two other field marks, which experienced gull observers notice right away: legs and eyes. Study W93 and explain all the marks that can be used to distinguish one of these species from the others.

_____

_____

_____

_____

_____

_____

With this analysis of the larger gulls out of the way, you've done the hard work. You're ready to go out and start observing the details we've discussed here.

CHAPTER 16

Sparrows

Many beginning birders tend to pass over sparrows with a sigh and a shrug, as if they are all just little brown jobs that are too confusing to examine seriously. True, they are all little, and largely brown, but they also sport beautiful patterns of rust, black, white, gray, and orange, and more than one artist has been moved by their beauty to study the sparrows and paint them all. As you learn to see the features of birds clearly, you'll see how wonderfully varied the sparrows are and how really easy it can be to separate and enjoy them. You will come to appreciate the rusty cap and bright white supercilium of a little Chipping Sparrow; the harlequin face of a Lark Sparrow; the auricular patch of a Clay-colored Sparrow; the dazzlingly brilliant orange face of a Nelson's Sharp-tailed Sparrow lit by the prairie sun.

Although sparrows in the broad sense include the towhees, longspurs, and some buntings, I am restricting the analysis here to more typical little brownish birds. One preliminary issue is the problem of the little brown female finches, alluded to earlier. We've already touched on the streaked females, including the female Rose-breasted Grosbeak and the female *Carpodacus* finches (House, Purple, Cassin's), which have large bills and heavy streaking all over their undersides. A few sparrows have such streaking: Song, Savannah, Fox, Vesper, Lincoln's. I think we have to acknowledge that distinguishing these female finches from the sparrows is a problem of more advanced birding, to be sorted out largely by experience. Second, the female small buntings — Painted, Lazuli, Indigo — are plain brown above and mottled tan brown below (E289; W339) and the female Blue Grosbeak is similar but larger. *No sparrow looks like this* except the female House Sparrow. House Sparrows are an Old World sparrow (Passeridae, E319; W347), not a true, patriotic, upstanding American sparrow (Embirizidae).

EXERCISE 16-1. You are most likely to know female House Sparrows by their association with obvious males and their human-associated habitat (cities, farm buildings), and distinguishing them from the female finches may be a minor task for the future, but there are a few field marks to help you make the distinction. What are they?

_____

_____

_____

_____

Before you look at the different species of sparrows, it will help to know something about sparrow biology in general. Sparrows hatched during the spring and summer soon develop juvenal plumage, which is always streaked. No, this is not a misspelling; *juvenal plumage* properly refers to the plumage of a juvenile bird. It lasts for only a few months and is replaced in late summer or early fall by the first basic plumage, which resembles adult plumage but isn't as bright and has a yellowish or buffy cast. I don't believe it is worthwhile for beginners to pay much attention to these plumages. Learning about basic (winter) plumages that are distinct from typical adult breeding plumages certainly goes well beyond beginning. Wait until you've become comfortable with the more common adult sparrows, even though that means you'll see sparrows that you just can't identify yet. A second way to simplify your introduction to sparrows is to *skip over some western sparrows* that are a bit too obscure or confined in range for rank beginners to deal with at first: Botteri's, Rufous-winged, Five-striped, and Black-chinned.

A somewhat more serious issue in sparrow biology is the degree of geographic variation in several species, in some cases great enough that many authorities believe the birds currently counted as a single species should really be divided into two or more. But we'll address this only to the extent that it's covered by the Peterson guides.

Sparrows are clearly divided into those with streaked breasts and those with plain breasts, and then into a few well-defined groups:

Clear-breasted sparrows:

Genus *Zonotrichia*: large, long-bodied sparrows with generally plain grayish breasts
Genus *Spizella* and their kin: the rusty-capped sparrows
Genus *Chondestes*: the Lark Sparrow
Genus *Amphispiza*: the Sage, "Bell's," and Black-throated Sparrows
Genus *Aimophila*: Bachman's and Cassin's Sparrows

Streak-breasted sparrows:

Genus *Melospiza* and their kin: large to medium-sized sparrows, often quite
    rusty
Genus *Ammodramus*: the little "flat-heads"

The Zonotrichias

The *Zonotrichia (zo-no-TRIK-ee-uh)* sparrows stand out through the combination of a clear breast, a typical head pattern, and size — generally about 7 inches long, which is large for a sparrow. They are quite common at certain times and places, so it will help to ask yourself the GLQ. For that purpose, examine the range maps for these sparrows and answer these questions.

EXERCISE 16-2. Where are Golden-crowned Sparrows found?

EXERCISE 16-3. Where are Harris's Sparrows found?

The point of these questions is that Americans generally see these two species only in the winter and only in limited locales, although they can turn up accidentally anywhere. Notice that the Harris's Sparrow breaks the mold with its black crown and face, a pattern that makes it stand out and be instantly identifiable, even in its winter plumage.

EXERCISE 16-4. Examine the plates of the *Zonotrichias* (E295; W317) and do a diagnosis of the group.

The *Spizellas* and One *Melospiza*

The rusty-capped sparrows are of a more typical sparrow size, 5–6 inches long. Their very existence means that one of the first things to notice about a sparrow is *whether it has such a rusty cap*. Over most of the continent, the species to be concerned about are the Chipping, Field, Swamp, and Tree Sparrows, as well as the Rufous-crowned Sparrow of the Southwest and southern plains (but not Rufous-winged). We encounter Chipping and Field Sparrows in open fields and brushy edges. Wetter territory yields Swamp Sparrows.

EXERCISE 16-5. Use the range maps (map E387; map W384) to answer this question: Other than in the far north, when and where will you see Tree Sparrows?

_____

EXERCISE 16-6. Do a diagnosis of the rusty-crowned species.

_____

_____

_____

_____

_____

_____

_____

_____

EXERCISE 16-7. We need to pay attention to an unusual *Spizella*, the Clay-colored Sparrow. Examine this sparrow (E299; W323) and explain how to recognize it.

_____

EXERCISE 16-8. How can you distinguish a Clay-colored Sparrow from a Chipping Sparrow in their winter plumage (E297)?

_____

_____

_____

Lark Sparrow

EXERCISE 16-9. Look at a Lark Sparrow (E299; W319). This species is placed in a separate genus, and is it any wonder? With that distinctive facial pattern, it can't be confused with any other sparrow. What are two other field marks that will help you recognize it?

_____

_____

_____

Amphispizas: Sage, "Bell's," and Black-throated Sparrows

Two of the sparrows shown on W319 are common inhabitants of the arid brush and deserts of the West. Throughout the Great Basin region (map W393) you will find the lovely little gray Sage Sparrows in brushy territory among the sagebrush and rabbit brush, usually foraging on the ground, and when startled they will run with their tails up in the air. You will know them by two field marks: a black spot in the center of the clear breast and heavy black malar stripes.

The similar sparrows that inhabit a narrow band along coastal California have been considered a subspecies of the Sage Sparrow, but many authorities now consider them a distinct species called Bell's Sparrow. Notice how similar they are to Sage Sparrows, with dark brown backs instead of gray and with much heavier malar stripes.

In the southwestern deserts (map W392), the little Black-throated Sparrows will pop out at you, and their black throats are so obvious that you can hardly mistake them for anything else.

EXERCISE 16-10. Well, hardly anything else. Look at Harris's Sparrows, House Sparrow males, and Black-throated Sparrows, and explain how to separate them by the difference in their prominent black patches.

_____

_____

_____

_____

Aimophilas: Bachman's and Cassin's Sparrows

Some sparrows of the genus _Aimophila (aim-AH-fil-uh)_ are in that list of obscure species that I suggest you leave aside for now, and Cassin's could be in the list, too. How can we characterize sparrows that virtually lack characteristics? First, you have to be in the right place to see this species, an area of dry shortgrass prairie in the southern Great Plains. Second, the _Aimophilas_ are sparrows with rounded tails, whereas most others have tails with flat or notched ends. Third, you may see a sparrow with virtually none of the distinctive field marks of other species: no rusty cap, no auricular patch, no strong eye line or eyebrow, no malar stripe. It has whitish tips on the outer tail feathers — gee, that's really an outstanding feature, isn't it? Well, this drab little sparrow is a Cassin's. The bird is known to sing a beautiful song, often in flight, described as _see-tzeeeeee-tee-a-zhreeee._

Bachman's _(BACK-mans)_ Sparrow is similar, with dingy buff stripes on its breast and somewhat stronger crown stripes than Cassin's. It is a shy little sparrow of certain localities in the open pinewoods scrub of the South; as Peterson notes, it flushes reluctantly and then drops into cover. Bachman's Sparrows are most easily seen during the breeding season, when the males sing persistently from exposed perches not far from the ground.

Melospizas and Other Rusty Streak-Breasted Sparrows

The species known largely by their heavily streaked breasts are the Song and Lincoln's Sparrows of the genus _Melospiza (mel-oh-SPY-zah)_, and the similar Fox, Savannah, and Vesper Sparrows in genera of their own. Song and Fox Sparrows are easy to recognize in one sense — that they have prominent field marks — but are difficult in another sense: Extreme geographic variation means that birds of the same species in different parts of the continent look quite different.

Fox Sparrows vary so much that many ornithologists believe the species ought to be divided into four species. Eastern North America has only the "Red" Fox Sparrow, with bright rusty tail and wings (E301), whose breeding range extends broadly across Canada and interior Alaska. In the West, you may occasionally see a "Red" Sparrow, but you are more likely to see one of the forms Peterson shows on W325. The "Sooty" Fox Sparrow breeds from the Aleutian Islands and coastal Alaska south to northwestern Washington; the "Slate-colored" form breeds in the Rocky Mountains and other mountains of the West; and the "Thick-billed" breeds from the northern Oregon Cascades to southern California. That may seem to be more information than you need as a beginner, but it will help you make sense of the forms shown in the plate and prepare you for what you are most likely to see.

EXERCISE 16-11. In spite of these variations, what general features of Fox Sparrows will help you recognize them?

_____

_____

_____

Song Sparrows are very common — Pete Dunne calls this species the "default sparrow" — and they vary geographically much like Fox Sparrows, although they are clearly a single species. Song Sparrows throughout most of the East (E301) are easily recognized by their long rounded tails and breast stripes converging to a central spot. Western subspecies, however, vary a lot (W325) and may not show the breast spot clearly, so we have to supplement the central breast spot by noting a white throat bordered with heavy black malar stripes and a white or slightly off-white eyebrow. Song Sparrows also have a characteristic flight — bouncy, with tail pumping — which you can learn through careful field observation.

Let's compare Song Sparrows with three similar species. Savannah Sparrows also show considerable geographic variation. Birders may go out of their way to observe the "Ipswich" form of the East (E303) or the California coastal forms (W327). But let's concentrate on the more typical form.

EXERCISE 16-12. Do both Song Sparrows and Savannah Sparrows have:

(a) a white throat bordered by malar stripes? _____

(b) a white or off-white eyebrow? _____

(c) a longish tail with a rounded tip?

Aha! So now we have at least two good marks for distinguishing Song Sparrows from Savannahs. Peterson notes that not all Savannahs have the yellowish eyebrow, but most do, and I think it is generally the most obvious field mark.

EXERCISE 16-13. Now compare Song and Lincoln's Sparrows. (Lincoln's has a shorter tail, flat to round on the end, but that's not a very critical field mark.) Compare the breast streaking of Lincoln's and Song Sparrows, the colors of the eyebrow, and the extent of the buffy color on Lincoln's. Now, what makes Lincoln's stand out?

_____

_____

_____

In fact, the Lincoln's is a beautiful little sparrow, with its combination of a gray face and the buffy color that comes up into the area just above the malar stripe.

EXERCISE 16-14. We've already dealt with the Swamp Sparrow, another *Melospiza*, which has that distinctive rusty cap. The remaining sparrow to examine closely along with Song, Savannah, and Lincoln's Sparrows is the Vesper Sparrow. All these species are similar, but you should be able to find at least three field marks of a Vesper Sparrow.

_____

_____

_____

Before leaving these streaked sparrows, it is worth considering some aspects of their habitats and behaviors, as these can also be important in recognizing them. Song Sparrows seem to live wherever there is brushy edge habitat, which they readily leave while feeding, so we commonly see them hopping along in open spaces that some other species avoid. Lincoln's, as Peterson notes, is "a skulker, afraid of its shadow." It tends to stay in brushy areas, especially wet areas, rather than coming out in the open. The Savannah is a grassland species, even if *grassland* means only the open edge of a woods or the border of a road; it is a sociable species, often found in small flocks of its own kind but not with other species. The Vesper is also a bird of the grasslands that will feed in the open, far from cover; it is also a sociable species, and in contrast to the Savannah it may join flocks with other species of sparrows. Fox Sparrows prefer the undergrowth of wooded areas, where we commonly see them on the ground among the leaf litter, scratching away, overturning leaves, and even digging holes.

The *Ammodramus* Sparrows

These are small sparrows of the prairie grasses or of marshes (sometimes, prairie marshes) with a typically *flat-headed* look; that is, a typical bird has a low crown, so its forehead runs directly into its bill almost in a straight line. The genus *Ammodramus (am-ODD-ra-mus)* includes Grasshopper, Henslow's, Baird's, Le Conte's, Seaside, and two species of Sharp-tailed Sparrows (split in 1995 from a single species). It is helpful to separate these birds on the basis of their habitats, because you generally need to travel to certain designated places to find them, either on the prairies or in coastal marshes.

The grassland sparrows are Grasshopper, Baird's, and Henslow's (E299, 303; W323, 327). Read the texts regarding these species and look at their range maps (maps E396, 397, 398; maps W396, 397). One of their characteristics is being in some trouble as a species because of increasing agricultural incursions into their habitats, and the very specific habitat requirements of Henslow's Sparrows put them in even greater danger than the others. I point this out to make it clear that you aren't going to be confronted with these birds if you casually stroll into a woodland or meadow where you might expect Song or other common sparrows. To see them, you will probably have to take a special trip to one of the isolated areas where they still breed. (I found Grasshopper and Baird's Sparrows only by taking a guided trip to some spots in North Dakota wildlife refuges at an American Birding Association convention.)

EXERCISE 16-15. Even though it may be hard to locate the Grasshopper, Baird's, and Henslow's Sparrows, do a diagnosis of their field marks. Notice that adult Grasshopper Sparrows have weak breast stripes.

_____

_____

_____

_____

_____

EXERCISE 16-16. The *Ammodramus* sparrows of the marshes — Seaside, Salt-marsh Sharp-tailed, Nelson's Sharp-tailed, and Le Conte's — have plumages that separate them from others of the genus, and they are generally easier to locate. Examine their plumage (E305; W327), noting that older field guides don't separate the two species of Sharp-tails. To me, the wonderful characteristic of most of these birds is their bright ocher or orange coloration; as fine as Peterson's plates are, they cannot convey the beauty of the real bird viewed in good sunlight. Do a diagnosis of these species.

_____

_____

_____

_____

_____

_____

_____

CHAPTER 17

Fun and Games

This book has attempted to guide you along a threefold path, the primary lessons being that you must keep striving to *see* — to really see the critical features of a bird when you look at it; to learn to put birds into categories, ranging from orders to genera; and to start learning the easiest birds first. So now it's time to repeat an admonition from chapter 1: This takes time. It really takes a lifetime, and all birders are continually striving to see birds more clearly, more precisely, more distinctly.

Remember that birding is supposed to be fun. You're supposed to do it for pleasure, for excitement, for adventure. Now I suggest that one of the best ways to advance and to learn birds better is to play games. Once you get the idea, you can undoubtedly make up a lot of new games, so I'll describe just a few of them here.

Game 1: Call It

You can play this game alone as a learning device, or a small group can play it together. The following pages have information about the American wood warblers, the Parulidae. They can be cut up to make a set of cards with the name of a species on one side and some of its field marks on the other side. With a small group, one person takes the deck of cards and begins to read off the field marks one at a time. The first person to correctly name the species wins that round. You can keep track of the number of correct identifications each one makes. The reader can read the clues in different orders if he or she thinks it will be more challenging. It doesn't take a lot of work to extend the game to other groups by making sets of similar cards for them. Of course, you don't even have to restrict it to one family; mix up all the North American passerines if you want to.

Yellow throat and
upper breast

White wing bars

Gray back

Black eyeline and
auricular leading
to black streaks
on flanks

White belly

Gray-white
streaked body

Black face and ear

Yellow crown patch

Yellow rump

Black breast-band

Yellow throat

Yellow patch below
wing

Yellow throat

Yellow breast and
belly

Black side streaks

Black streak
through eye

Black malar stripe

Streaked olive
back

Faint wing bars

Yellow throat

Yellow breast

Plain olive back
and wings

Gray head

White eye-ring

No wing bars

Yellow throat

White wing bars

Gray back with
green patch

Dark band with
orange on breast

White eye
crescents

Yellow throat

Gray back and
wings

No wing bars

Yellow underparts

Yellow spectacles

Necklace of black
stripes

Yellow throat

Yellow breast and
belly

White eyebrow

Chestnut cap

Streaked olive
back

No wing bars

Light side streaks

Plain olive back
and wings

Gray head

White eyebrow

White throat,
breast, and belly

Yellow throat and
head

Head and breast
all yellow to
orange

Olive back

Blue-gray wings

No wing bars

Yellow throat

Yellow underparts
streaked with
black

Wide white wing
bars, almost a
patch

Streaked yellowish
back

Yellow rump

Chestnut auricular

Yellow throat

Yellow breast

Yellow belly

Unstreaked olive
back

Bluish wing with
white wing bars

Black line through
eye

Plain olive green
back

Greenish yellow
underparts

Faint breast
streaks

No wing bars

Almost invisible
orange crown

Yellow throat

Yellow underparts
with heavy black
streaks

Gray crown

White wing patch
or wing bars

Yellow rump

White band in tail

Yellow throat

Yellow breast

Unstreaked olive
back

White wing bars,
prominent

Faint streaks at
side of breast

Yellow throat

Yellow breast

Yellow belly

Rusty red breast
streaks

Olive-yellow back

Yellow streaks in
tail

Yellow throat and
face

Yellow breast

Yellow belly

Round black cap

Unstreaked olive
back and wings

No wing bars

Nashville Warbler	Prairie Warbler	Yellow-rumped "Audubon's" Warbler	Yellow-throated Warbler
Tennessee Warbler	Palm Warbler	Canada Warbler	Northern Parula
Orange-crowned Warbler	Blue-winged Warbler	Cape May Warbler	Prothonotary Warbler
Wilson's Warbler	Yellow Warbler	Pine Warbler	Magnolia Warbler

Black-and-white body

Bright orange on head and throat

Black auricular

Black streaks on sides

White wing patch

All black-and-white streaks

Streaked greenish back

Black crown

Gray streaked wings with wing bars

White cheeks

Black throat

Black hood

Yellow face

Yellow belly

Plain olive back and wings

Black throat

Black breast extending to sides

Plain olive back and crown

White wing bars

Bright yellow face and auricular

Grayish streaked body

Chestnut to brown throat, head, and sides

Buff neck patch

White wing bars

Streaked back

Gray-black hood

No eye-ring

Yellow belly

Black breast patch

Plain olive back

No wing bars

Black throat

Black breast

Black head

Black back

Orange patches in wings and tail

Black throat

All black-and-white streaks

White wing bars

Black streaked back

Black auricular

White throat and underparts

Yellow crown

White auricular

Chestnut sides and flanks

Black-streaked yellowish back

Medium gray hood

White eye-ring

Yellow belly

Plain olive back and wings

No wing bars

White throat and undersides

Black streaks on sides

Narrow black bar across breast

Blue head and back streaked with black

Gray-white streaked body

Black face and ear

Yellow crown patch

Yellow rump

Black breast

White throat

Yellow patch below wing

Yellow throat

Yellow breast

Plain olive back

Black mask over face and ears

Black throat

Gray back

Black patch through eye and cheek

Yellow wing patch

Yellow cap

Black face surrounded by white

White belly

Black throat

Black face

Black sides

Small white patch on wing

Deep blue back

Yellow throat

Yellow breast

Yellow belly

Black sideburns below eye

Yellow spectacles

Plain olive back

Black-throated Green Warbler	Hooded Warbler	Blackpoll Warbler	Blackburnian Warbler
Black-and-white Warbler	American Redstart	Mourning Warbler	Bay-breasted Warbler
Yellow-rumped Warbler	Cerulean Warbler	Connecticut Warbler	Chestnut-sided Warbler
Kentucky Warbler	Black-throated Blue Warbler	Golden-winged Warbler	Common Yellowthroat

Game 2: Where Am I?

Each person can prepare for the game by studying places in North America and making lists of distinctive species found there at certain times of the year. The more places, the better, of course. Each person can then challenge the others. First identify the time of year for the spot you've chosen, and then start reading the list of species found there. The first person to correctly name the spot wins that round.

Game 3: Bird Songs

Using various CDs of bird songs and your own electronic devices — there are so many that I wouldn't dare suggest the best method — make your own recordings of songs without the identifying labels. Keep a list of the songs, and play the recordings for the group. For competition, keep track of who can name the most species.

Game 4: Test My Memory

This can be a simple game you play alone just to become more familiar with a lot of birds, or you can play it with others as a challenge game. The game is simply to name all the birds that:

a. have yellow breasts crossed by a black V
b. show white outer tail feathers
c. hunt by hovering
d. have white rump or tail patches
e. have a white patch of some kind on the wings (not wing bars)
f. have crested heads
g. have deeply forked tails

and so on. There's no limit to such a list, and as you learn more, you can extend it to behaviors, habitats, ways of constructing nests, and other traits.

Answers to Exercises

EXERCISE 2-1 (p. 16). Insect eaters have small thin bills. Seed eaters have strong conical bills, and those with a mixed diet of seeds and insects have somewhat conical bills for eating seeds but modified for eating insects. More omnivorous birds have substantial bills of other shapes, and shrikes, which eat birds and mammals, have hooked bills similar to those of hawks.

EXERCISE 2-2 (p. 22). Blackbird's tail has a round tip; cowbird's is slightly notched.

EXERCISE 2-3 (p. 22). Goldfinch and Pine Siskin have slightly notched tails; sparrows such as Song, Lincoln's, and Swamp have rounded tails.

EXERCISE 2-4 (p. 22). Blackbirds' tails are fairly short, with tips that are flat or slightly notched; grackles have long tails with round ends.

EXERCISE 2-5 (p. 22). Meadowlarks have white outer tail feathers, very obvious from behind, especially as a bird flies away. Dickcissel has a plain brown tail with an essentially flat tip; Bobolink's tail is rounded and a buffy color.

EXERCISE 2-6 (p. 22). Almost all gulls have fan-shaped, round tails; almost all terns have forked tails.

EXERCISE 2-7 (p. 23). Black-billed Cuckoos have small white crescents only at the tips of their tail feathers; Yellow-billed Cuckoos show large patches of white.

EXERCISE 2-8 (p. 23). Crows' tails are fan-shaped; raven's tail is wedge-shaped, broadening out and then narrowing to a round (almost pointed) end.

EXERCISE 2-9 (p. 23). Spruce Grouse has a rounded black and chestnut tail; Sharp-tailed Grouse has a pointed tail; Prairie Chickens have rounded black tails with no chestnut.

EXERCISE 2-10 (p. 23). Orioles are long and slim, have long tails with round ends, and bills that are long, narrow, sharply pointed, and curved slightly downward. Tanagers are chunkier, have shorter tails with slightly notched ends, and large, heavy bills.

EXERCISE 3-1 (p. 30). While this is the kind of question you have to answer for yourself, notice that wading birds such as herons and egrets stand very much erect and vertical, whereas ducks sit in the water in horizontal orientations. Similarly, owls and woodpeckers tend to stand vertically; hawks are almost vertical when perched. Most shorebirds have quite horizontal bodies.

EXERCISE 3-2 (p. 30). Your answers to this question, also, are necessarily personal, because there is no clear division between large and small. However, most herons and egrets are quite large, and we probably think of ducks and hawks as largish birds. Hummingbirds are obviously tiny, and most passerines are small. You'll eventually see that some orders include birds of quite different sizes; we might think of owls, for instance, as large birds, and many are, but there are also very tiny owls.

EXERCISE 3-3 (p. 31). The curved bills of hawks and owls are used for tearing flesh; herons and egrets use their spearlike bills for catching fish, frogs, and other small animals.

EXERCISE 3-4 (p. 31). Chickenlike birds eat seeds and grain.

EXERCISE 3-5 (p. 31). Gulls and terns live around water. Terns eat fish or other aquatic animals. Gulls eat everything, including carrion and garbage.

EXERCISE 3-6 (p. 40). Loons are large-bodied birds with moderately long necks and gently rounded curves from the backs of the heads into the necks. Their bills are pointed and spearlike, in contrast to the flattened bills of ducks. Grebes have longer necks than typical ducks, with spearlike bills similar to those of loons but generally thinner. Unlike loons, they typically have a squareness to the back of the head.

1. (p. 41). Dabbling duck

2. (p. 41). Coots

3. (p. 41). Cormorant

4. (p. 41). Diving duck

5. (p. 41). A dabbler

6. (p. 41). Diving duck

7. (p. 41). A dabbler

8. (p. 42). Dive

9. (p. 42). Merganser; bill has sawtooth edges, used for catching fish

10. (p. 42). Bufflehead and Hooded Merganser; Bufflehead's patch is plain, but the merganser's patch is on its hood, surrounded by a black edge.

11. (p. 42). A grebe

12. (p. 42). Bufflehead, Common Merganser

13. (p. 42). Female Bufflehead

14. (p. 42). Goldeneye

15. (p. 43). Green-winged teal

CHAPTER 4 QUIZ

1. (p. 52) Great Blue Heron

2. (p. 52) Killdeer

3. (p. 52) Mourning Dove

4. (p. 52) Ruby-throated Hummingbird

5. (p. 52) Downy Woodpecker

6. (p. 53) Blue Jay

7. (p. 53) Steller's Jay

8. (p. 53) Black-billed Magpie

9. (p. 53) Barn Swallow

10. (p. 53) Brown Creeper

11. (p. 53) White-breasted Nuthatch

12. (p. 53) Eastern Bluebird

13. (p. 53) Mockingbird

14. (p. 54) Brown Thrasher

15. (p. 54) Northern Cardinal

16. (p. 54) Western Meadowlark

17. (p. 54) Red-winged Blackbird

18. (p. 54) Yellow-headed Blackbird

19. (p. 54) Common Grackle

20. (p. 54) Rose-breasted Grosbeak

21. (p. 54) Scarlet Tanager

22. (p. 55) American Goldfinch

23. (p. 55) House Sparrow

EXERCISE 5-1 (p. 58). White median crown stripe, chestnut (brown) lateral crown stripes, white supercilium (eyebrow), black eye line (or black line in lores), chestnut auricular, slight black mustachial stripe, white submustachial stripe, black malar stripe, white throat.

EXERCISE 5-2 (p. 59). White median crown stripe, brown lateral crown stripes, white supercilium (eyebrow), buffy tan auricular, slight black mustachial and malar stripes, white submustachial stripe, gray nape (collar).

EXERCISE 5-3 (p. 59). Mottled greenish black crown and center of nape; yellow eyebrow; rusty auricular; yellow chin, extending to sides of nape; breast and sides yellow with black streaks.

EXERCISE 5-4 (p. 59). Least has a strong eye-ring, Alder a much weaker eye-ring, and Western has a tear-shaped eye-ring.

EXERCISE 5-5 (p. 59). Strong white supercilium (eyebrow).

EXERCISE 5-6 (p. 60). Red-eyed Vireo has a strong white eyebrow, outlined above and below by black lines; Warbling Vireo has a fainter eyebrow with no such black lines. (Looking at the Field Guide plate, you may also note the vireo's red eye; this is generally hard to see in the field.)

EXERCISE 5-7 (p. 60). Magnolia male: crown gray, short white superciliary, black lores and auricular (ear patch), yellow chin and throat, black line about where throat and breast meet, breast yellow with heavy black streaks on sides. Yellow-rumped ("Myrtle"): differs from Magnolia in having yellow patch on crown, very thin white eyebrow, white chin and throat, much broader black band on breast, which is white except for heavy black streaking on sides and yellow side patch. Yellow-rumped Audubon's differs in having yellow chin and throat, black auricular replaced by solid gray, breast even more completely black.

Females: female Magnolia differs from male in having lighter black streaks on breast. (And while the instructions were to concentrate on the head and breast, note that white wing patch of male is replaced by two wing bars in female.)

Female Myrtle differs from male in having gray auricular rather than black, much lighter black streaking on breast. Female Audubon's differs from male in having smaller yellow crown patch, much lighter yellow on chin and throat, much lighter gray on head, breast with light gray streaking rather than intense black.

EXERCISE 5-8 (p. 61). Townsend's: black crown and auricular, yellow supercilium and malar stripe, black chin and throat, yellow breast with black streaking on sides. Hermit: black back of crown, but front of crown and auricular replaced by yellow, making solid yellow side of head. Breast white instead of yellow, no side streaking.

Females: Townsend's female a paler version of male, with gray auricular, little black on throat. Similarly, Hermit female resembles male but with less extensive black on throat.

EXERCISE 5-9 (p. 61). Two eye crescents rather than a complete eye-ring.

EXERCISE 5-10 (p. 61). All three sparrows have strongly streaked heads; White-throated and White-crowned have white median crown stripes, black lateral crown stripes, and white eyebrow, though notice that in the White-throated the eyebrow extends all the way in front of the eye to a yellow spot, whereas the White-crowned has shorter white eyebrow and black in the lores. Of course, the White-throated has a white throat patch. Golden-crowned has a yellow median line with strong black on the eyebrow and eye line. Note the pink bill of the White-crowned. In the field, if you can't see the bill and throat of a possible White-throated, you would want to concentrate on the pattern of head stripes, especially the median stripe.

EXERCISE 5-11 (p. 62). The Goshawk has strong black-and-white head stripes, especially a white eyebrow; the Cooper's has only a mottled black and gray head, with something of a black crown.

EXERCISE 5-12 (p. 62). Connecticut: full gray hood with a distinct white eye-ring. Nashville: only a partial hood, with the crown and nape a light gray, and a yellow throat; also has a white eye-ring. Mourning: full hood with black on the breast, but no eye-ring. MacGillivray's: full hood, even darker than that of Connecticut, but only a partial eye-ring, broken into eye crescents.

EXERCISE 5-13 (p. 63). The primaries.

EXERCISE 5-14 (p. 64). Cape May and Chestnut-sided: broad white wing bars that blend with each other. Bay-breasted: two distinct white wing bars. Blackburnian: a single white wing patch. Redstart: a bright orange wing patch.

EXERCISE 5-15 (p. 64). American Tree Sparrows and Field Sparrows have two strong wing bars. Chipping Sparrows have slight wing bars. Swamp and Rufous-crowned Sparrows have no wing bars. Juvenile Chipping Sparrows have no wing bars and gain them as they molt into adult plumage; adults then lose their wing bars in winter plumage.

EXERCISE 5-16 (p. 64). Catbirds have plain gray wings with no markings, Brown Thrashers have two strong white wing bars, and Mockingbirds have two strong wing bars and a white patch on a streaky gray and white background.

EXERCISE 5-17 (p. 65). Eastern Phoebes have no wing bars. Eastern and Western Wood-Pewees both have narrow white wing bars.

EXERCISE 5-18 (p. 65). Both species have streaky black-and-white wings. Baltimore male has one prominent white wing bar, Bullock's male has a large white wing patch.

CHAPTER 6 QUIZ

1. (p. 73) Sparrow

2. (p. 73) Warbler

3. (p. 73) Flycatcher

4. (p. 73) Sparrow

5. (p. 73) Kinglet

6. (p. 73) Blackbird

7. (p. 74) Thrush

8. (p. 74) Thrush

9. (p. 74) Warbler

10. (p. 74) Vireo

11. (p. 74) Flycatcher

12. (p. 74) Oriole

13. (p. 75) Thrush

14. (p. 75). Chickadee

15. (p. 75). Sparrow

16. (p. 75). Cuckoo

17. (p. 75). Kinglet

18. (p. 76). Rail

19. (p. 76). Wren

20. (p. 76). Flycatcher

21. (p. 76). Kingfisher

22. (p. 76). Warbler

23. (p. 77). Woodpecker

24. (p. 77). Vireo

25. (p. 77). Alcids

EXERCISE 8-1 (p. 86). Look for prominent white wing bars. Yes: White-winged. No: Red.

EXERCISE 8-2 (p. 86). Here's one solution: Is the bird blue over the entire body? (The alternative is having different colors on the wings or underparts.) If so, it is either the medium blue color of an Indigo Bunting or the deep, dark blue of a Blue Bunting, a rare Texas specialty. Alternatively, if the bird has brown wing bars and a large grosbeak bill, it is a Blue Grosbeak. If it has white wing bars, a cinnamon breast, and white underparts, it is a Lazuli Bunting.

EXERCISE 8-3 (p. 86). Look for Northern Shrike's faint breast streaks, a mask interrupted over the bill, and a light base of the lower mandible; all three are good field marks, though subtle. Loggerhead's mask is solid black over the bill, and the bill is all black.

EXERCISE 8-4 (p. 86). One solution: Look first for a prominent black-white-black eyebrow, to separate out the Red-eyed and Black-whiskered, then differentiate by presence or absence of the black whisker line. The alternative is a plain white eyebrow; then Philadelphia is told by its yellowish underparts and black loral spot, which the Warbling Vireo lacks. Alternatively, consider the yellowish underparts first, especially if you want to include the Yellow-green Vireo. For the West, do the same analysis but at some point note that the Gray Vireo has no eyebrow at all but has a thin eye-ring on a gray face.

EXERCISE 8-5 (p. 87). One solution is to first separate out the Barn Swallow, with its long swallowtail feathers. The Violet-green stands out because it flashes white patches on the sides of the rump, and the male Purple Martin stands out because overall it is dark blue-black and rather heavy. At this point, you might separate the Cliff Swallow because of its squarish tail and buffy rump. The remaining species have slightly forked tails, and you might distinguish the Tree Swallow, with its blue-green back and clear white breast and belly, from the others, which have brown backs. Then the Bank Swallow has an obvious breast-band, and the Rough-winged has a dusky throat.

EXERCISE 8-6 (p. 88). First, distinguish two species that are zebra-striped all over, including the face, from the two that have gray-tan undersides. For the first two, distinguish the Nuttall's, with a black nape and found west of the Sierras, from Ladder-backed, with a white nape and found east of the Sierras. For the second two, distinguish the Golden-fronted, with prominent orange patches on the nape and near the lores, from the Gila, which lacks such patches. Also, note the difference in their ranges.

EXERCISE 8-7 (p. 88). I separate three principal groups. (1) Mostly black, brown, white and gray, including Black-throated Gray, which has only those colors, and Yellow-rumped, which shows flashes of yellow from the rump and sides. (2) Show much yellow but aren't *all* yellow; includes Yellowthroat and MacGillivray's. Prominent black face mask marks a ♂ Yellowthroat; prominent slate gray hood marks a ♂ MacGillivray's; pale gray (dirty white) hood marks ♀ MacGillivray's; yellow on breast and a white belly marks ♀ Yellowthroat. (3) Essentially yellow all over, even just a dingy yellow; a small black cap identifies ♂ Wilson's, and having rusty breast streaks on a bright yellow body identifies ♂ Yellow Warbler. That leaves those that are just plain yellow. Yellow eyebrow (and perhaps a trace of a cap) identifies ♀ Wilson's; bright yellow with no eyebrow identifies ♀ Yellow; dingy yellow with no obvious marks identifies Orange-crowned.

EXERCISE 12-1 (p. 110). Pileated: female has no red on malar stripe, less red at front of crest.

Northern Flicker: female has no mustaches, red or black.

Downy and Hairy: females have no red at back of head.

Red-bellied: female has red at back of head only, not over entire cap.

Yellow-bellied Sapsucker: female has a white throat instead of red.

Red-naped Sapsucker: female has white chin instead of red.

Nuttall's and Ladder-backed: females lack red crown patches.

EXERCISE 12-2 (p. 111). Warblers and vireos

EXERCISE 12-3 (p. 111). Behavior: warblers move constantly, are very nervous. Vireos are more sedate, hold still more. Bills: warbler bills are quite thin, vireo bills are a little heavier, have more of a curve in the ridge, and have a small hook at the tip.

EXERCISE 12-4 (p. 113). The icterids (Icteridae), characterized by a generally long overall gestalt and a long, sharp, downcurved bill.

EXERCISE 12-5 (p. 113). Bill shape, body shape, tail shape.

EXERCISE 12-6 (p. 114). Warblers and vireos have already been characterized by their bills and ways of moving. Tanagers have short heavy bills, orioles have icterid bills, both groups with considerable curve to their top ridges. Tanagers have compact bodies, orioles are slimmer, more elongated. Although size comparisons in the field can be tricky, notice that tanagers are somewhat larger than warblers (7 inches long, compared to 5–5½ inches) and that orioles are also larger: 6–7 inches for the Orchard Oriole, 7–8 inches for others. Tanager tails are short and slightly notched; oriole tails are longer and rounded at their tips.

EXERCISE 13-1 (p. 120), EXERCISE 13-2 (p. 120). Although the rufous red tail of an adult Red-tailed Hawk is an excellent field mark, it may be hard to see, and immature birds don't have it. The light breast contrasting with a darker belly-band is a distinctive field mark on a perched bird. For Broad-wings and Red-shouldered, look closely at the tail patterns, the coloration of the breast and belly, and see whether there is a distinct red shoulder. For the western birds, look for distinctive rufous colors on the tail, the breast, or the back.

EXERCISE 13-3 (p. 121), EXERCISE 13-4 (p. 121). The best general field mark for a light-morph Red-tail is the dark patagial bar at the front edge of the wings. For Broad-wings and Red-shouldered, pay most attention to the tails, while noticing the size of a Broad-wing compared to the other two species. In the West, notice the chest-band of the Swainson's, the contrast between the wing linings and the flight feathers, and the very long-tailed, light appearance of the Ferruginous, with a V formed by the dark legs.

EXERCISE 13-5 (p. 122). Osprey has a white belly, Rough-legged a dark belly. Osprey hunts on crooked wings over water, fishing; Rough-legged hunts on spread wings over land.

EXERCISE 13-6 (p. 123). Peregrine has a heavy mustache, compared to thin mustaches of other falcons.

EXERCISE 13-7 (p. 123). Banded tail of the Merlin, especially the heavy band near the tip of the tail.

EXERCISE 13-8 (p. 124). Heavy black patch on upper forewing of the White-tailed, standing out against the white body. Mississippi Kite is mostly gray with a black tail and dark wingtips.

CHAPTER 13 QUIZ

1. (p. 124). Accipiter

2. (p. 124). Falcon. Light facial markings and barred tail indicate it's a Peregrine Falcon.

3. (p. 125). Buteo

4. (p. 125). Heavy mustaches. Falcon. Peregrine Falcon

5. (p. 125). Buteo. Dark patagial bar; Red-tailed Hawk

6. (p. 125). Slim overall body, long tail, and small head identify it as an accipiter.

7. (p. 125). Accipiter. Probably a Cooper's because of rounded tail.

8. (p. 126). Light windows in the wings. This contrasts with dark (rusty) wing linings and body. Also strongly banded tail. Red-shouldered Hawk

9. (p. 126). Accipiter

10. (p. 126). Male Kestrel, because of its rufous body, black tail band, and gray wings

11. (p. 126). Tail bands, with the white bands wide; also light wings contrasted with dark body; Broad-winged Hawk

12. (p. 127). Long white tail contrasted with dark legs; Ferruginous Hawk

13. (p. 127). Dark breast-band; contrast between light wing linings and dark flight feathers. Swainson's Hawk

14. (p. 127). Red-shouldered Hawk, with wide dark stripes; and Broad-winged Hawk, with wide white stripes

15. (p. 128). Red-tailed Hawk

16. (p. 128). Turkey Vulture, Northern Harrier

EXERCISE 14-1 (p. 132). Peep have light or lightly streaked underparts and short bills. Dunlin have black belly patches and longer, slightly drooping bills.

EXERCISE 14-2 (p. 133). White breast and belly with black breast-bands, at least partial bands; sandy brown back.

EXERCISE 14-3 (p. 134). The color of the back — as Peterson noted, the color of dry sand (Piping) rather than the color of wet sand (Semipalmated).

EXERCISE 14-4 (p. 134). Snowy Plovers have all-black bills, black rather than yellow or orange legs, and a distinctive dark auricular (cheek) patch.

EXERCISE 14-5 (p. 134). Look at their heads. Black-bellied has a white crown, the two Golden-Plovers have dark crowns.

EXERCISE 14-6 (p. 135). American migrates almost entirely east of the Rockies; some Pacific birds winter along the southern Pacific Coast.

EXERCISE 14-7 (p. 135). The white neck stripe of the Pacific extends along the flanks; the American has black flanks.

EXERCISE 14-8 (p. 136). By their behavior. The plovers have typical pause-and-run plover behavior; the Sanderlings are always in motion, especially chasing waves.

EXERCISE 14-9 (p. 136). Tail with plain gray back: Wandering Tattler. (And notice the longer bill.) With both white wing stripe and white stripes in the back: Black Turnstone. The other two have only white wing stripes; the Surfbird has a broad white tail with a black tip, and the Rock Sandpiper has a black band down the middle of the tail.

EXERCISE 14-10 (p. 137).

FEATURE	CICONIIFORMS	TALL SHOREBIRDS
Bills:	Heavy, fish-catching bills; even ibises' bills are heavy to the end	Much thinner bills
Necks:	Most have either very long necks, which they can bend into S-curves, or no neck at all (night-herons, bitterns)	Short but distinct necks
Plumage:	Uniform gray, uniform white, or bright plumages (Glossy Ibis, Scarlet Ibis)	Mottled brownish plumages

EXERCISE 14-11 (p. 139). Whimbrels have distinct crown stripes. Also, when Long-billed Curlews fly, they show cinnamon wing linings.

EXERCISE 14-12 (p. 140). (a) Marbled has light buffy brown underparts, Hudsonian's are darker cinnamon brown. (b) Marbled has cinnamon wing linings; Hudsonian shows a stark pattern of black and white, especially a white tail with a black tip.

EXERCISE 14-13 (p. 141). Bills: Stilt's is long and slightly decurved, Upland's is middle length and straight, Buff-breasted bill is very short. Breast plumage: Stilt is heavily spotted with transverse bars, Upland is lightly spotted and brown, Buff-breasted is plain and buffy. Overall: Buff-breasted has a prominent black eye surrounded by buff, and shorter legs. Upland Sandpiper is medium-sized, with long tail and small head for its size, and a white eyebrow. Stilt Sandpiper has heavy transverse stripes below and a rusty cheek patch.

EXERCISE 14-14 (p. 142). White-rumped Sandpiper: small, streaked, with marks extending well onto the belly and flanks; has a white rump; long wings extend beyond tail.

EXERCISE 14-15 (p. 142). Baird's Sandpiper: brown buffy breast contrasts with white belly; long wings extend beyond tail.

EXERCISE 14-16 (p. 142). Pectoral Sandpiper: medium-sized, longer neck than others; streaked buffy breast ends in sharp line at white belly.

EXERCISE 15-1 (p. 144). Nearly pure white: Ivory
Light, silvery gray, almost white: Glaucous, Iceland
Light to medium gray: Black-legged Kittiwake, Herring, Ring-billed, California, Thayer's, others
Dark gray: Laughing, Franklin's, Western, Yellow-footed
Black: Great Black-backed

EXERCISE 15-2 (p. 145). Frosty tips: Glaucous, Iceland. Black tips: several species such as Herring, Ring-billed. White-black-white: Franklin's. White in contrast to gray mantle: Black-headed, Bonaparte's.

EXERCISE 15-3 (p. 146). White stripe separating the black tip from the mantle.

EXERCISE 15-4 (p. 146). Bonaparte's has a black ear patch; Laughing has a bit of a gray ear patch, but primarily a smudge on nape of the head.

EXERCISE 15-5 (p. 147). Lesser has yellow legs rather than pink.

EXERCISE 15-6 (p. 147). Both red and black spots on the bill, greenish legs, dark eye.

EXERCISE 15-7 (p. 148). Black ring on the bill of the Ring-billed, compared with the Herring's larger, red-spotted bill.

EXERCISE 15-8 (p. 148). Only Herring Gull has pink legs; California Gull has greenish legs; and Ring-billed Gull may also have yellow-green legs. Bills are distinctive: large and red-spotted (Herring), large and red-black spotted (California), ringed (Ring-billed), or smaller and plain yellow (Mew). Herring and Ring-billed have yellow eyes, California and Mew dark eyes.

EXERCISE 16-1 (p. 149). Unstreaked breast with streaked back, buffy superciliary stripe (eyebrow), single white wing bar.

EXERCISE 16-2 (p. 151). Golden-crowned breeds along the Pacific Coast in British Columbia and Alaska, winters in coastal Washington through California.

EXERCISE 16-3 (p. 151). Harris's breeds in the far northern plains to the Arctic, winters in Great Plains of the United States.

EXERCISE 16-4 (p. 151). Distinguish Harris's by its black face and throat. A yellow median crown stripe means Golden-crowned. Look for the head patterns of the other two, especially the lores, and check for a white throat. But don't be fooled by the tan-striped form of the White-throated.

EXERCISE 16-5 (p. 152). In the winter, across most of the United States except for the South, and only casually to the West Coast.

EXERCISE 16-6 (p. 152). Take into account the white supercilium of Chipping Sparrow and Swamp Sparrow, the Chippy's very clean and white, the Swamp's duller. Something of a black eye line on both, which just accentuates the Chippy's white stripe. Take into account the Swamp's facial pattern, especially the white throat, black-gray malar lines, and faint breast streaks. Field and Tree have only gray supercilium; Field has the pink bill and a light eye-ring. American Tree most likely to be seen during the winter, has its stickpin in the breast; and Tree is really big compared to Field and Chippy. Chippy, Field, and Tree all have wing bars; Swamp doesn't. In the Southwest, pay attention to the Rufous-crowned Sparrow, which resembles a Swamp in some ways but has a prominent black whisker.

EXERCISE 16-7 (p. 152). Notice its sharply outlined buffy ear patch.

EXERCISE 16-8 (p. 153). Clay-colored has a brown rump, Chippy has a gray rump.

EXERCISE 16-9 (p. 153). Its black tail with rounded white corners; the stickpin in its breast.

EXERCISE 16-10 (p. 154). Harris's Sparrow has black from the crown across the face and onto the throat. Male House Sparrow has the black patch next to white cheeks, while the Black-throated Sparrow has gray cheeks separated by distinct white stripes above and below (malar and supercilium).

EXERCISE 16-11 (p. 155). A large sparrow with a large bill, plain rusty or brown back (though eastern race has a streaked back) with rusty rump and tail, coarsely streaked underparts.

EXERCISE 16-12 (p. 155). (a) yes; (b) no — Savannah has a yellowish eyebrow; (c) no — Savannah has a shorter notched tail.

EXERCISE 16-13 (p. 156). Lincoln's has fine streaking on the breast, a gray eyebrow, a generally gray face, and a buffy color on the breast that comes up into the face.

EXERCISE 16-14 (p. 156). White outer tail feathers, which are very obvious; a whitish eye-ring; and perhaps the chestnut patch on the wing.

EXERCISE 16-15 (p. 157). For Grasshopper, note the *pale* median crown stripe and a breast without dark streaks that has only light buffy streaking. For Baird's, note the finely streaked breast-band and an *ocher* median crown stripe. For Henslow's, note the fine streaks across the breast and flanks, with an unstreaked olive face and neck; also note the reddish wings.

EXERCISE 16-16 (p. 158). For Seaside, note the long bill, yellow supraloral spot on the face, and dingy olive-gray color. For both Sharp-tails, note the deep ocher-yellow on the face around the gray cheek, with some distinct breast streaks separating the Saltmarsh from the maritime race of the Nelson's. For Le Conte's, note the ocher-yellow eyebrow and breast, black-striped head, and streaks only on the sides of the breast and flanks.

APPENDIX 2

Buying Binoculars

Excellent binoculars have become an essential tool of birding. This section will help you choose binoculars for yourself, but before you buy, it is important to *try the instrument yourself,* ideally in a variety of lighting conditions. Go out with experienced birders for a while, see what they are using, and perhaps ask to look through their glasses briefly — maybe when the group has paused for a lunch break — so you'll have access to a range of binoculars and you can experience them in actual field conditions. Also, the optical companies are generally well represented at the many birding festivals held all over the country, and this is a good opportunity to try different brands and ask questions of the product specialists, who are often very knowledgeable. You may even be able to pick up a bargain there.

GENERAL QUESTIONS. When you shop for binoculars, ask yourself some general questions about how you are going to use and treat them.

- If you have an expensive pair of binoculars, will you be afraid to take them with you?
- Do you plan to store the binoculars in your car so they will always be with you? Is your car going to be sitting mostly in the hot sun, or in cold, damp conditions?
- Can you carry them easily when hiking, biking, or cross-country skiing? Maybe you want a second, smaller pair for this.
- Do you plan to use them in extremely humid or wet environments? Then be sure you buy binoculars that are well sealed and, ideally, purged with nitrogen.

QUALITY. Quality is about the durability of the metal case, whether the binoculars are well sealed against moisture, and especially whether the lenses and prisms are made of good glass and are ground and polished carefully. The quality of an optical instrument is measured by its *resolution;* two points are said to be *resolved* if the instrument can separate them so they don't appear to be a single point. A fine microscope used in a research laboratory has excellent lenses and excellent resolution, compared with the toy microscopes you can buy for your child to fool around with, and the same is true for binoculars. Some discount and large chain stores will sell you binoculars for $25 to $50 that look wonderful but are probably a waste of money. If you have unlimited funds — and want to impress other birders in the bargain — you can spend $1,500 or more on glasses of excellent quality made by Swarovski, Leica, or Zeiss that are almost guaranteed to give you the best possible views of birds in even difficult lighting conditions. Most people can't afford to spend so much; typical birders content themselves with binoculars in the price range of $300 to $700 that perform perfectly well. However, the American Birding Association (ABA) sells the Bushnell Birder binoculars, which are adequate for beginners, for about $50, and other slightly better glasses for around $100.

The quality of the glass used for lenses and prisms is a major factor. Excellent modern binoculars use high-density glass, commonly BaK-4 barium crown glass. Cheap binoculars use much lower-density glass. You'll find information about the glass used in binoculars in the ABA sales catalog, but generally you can tell only by the price of the instrument. The dividing line is around $200 to $300. Above that line, you can be sure you're getting binoculars of good glass quality and can concentrate on other criteria.

Your optics must also be fully *coated*. When light passes from one medium to another, as between air and the glass of a prism or lens, some is lost by reflection. Low-reflection coatings (generally of magnesium fluoride, which gives the surface a purple color) increase the light transmitted, thus increasing contrast, reducing glare, and eliminating reflections. For best results, *all* glass surfaces at air-glass interfaces should be coated, and ideally they should be *multicoated,* which means the coating has been applied in several thin layers, reducing the light loss even more. You can notice the difference between single- and multicoatings particularly in a situation of extreme contrast, such as viewing birds in shade when there are also brightly lit objects in the field of view. For best results, insist on binoculars that are fully multicoated. Cheap binoculars often have coatings on only the outside surfaces, creating some color that may fool a naive buyer into thinking the binoculars are fully coated. For this reason alone, you should buy from a well-respected manufacturer and a reputable dealer.

BINOCULAR STYLE. All binoculars used for birding are *center-focus,* which means you focus them for different distances by turning a wheel in the center. Birders should avoid four types of binoculars that may look attractive but are no good for birding. First, stay away from *individual-focus* binoculars on which each eyepiece must be focused separately. Second, ignore any binoculars advertised as *permanent* or *fixed focus*; they force your eyes to do the focusing, and your eyes will soon get tired and give out on you. Third, there are binoculars advertised as "fast-focus" or "instant focus," which use a lever instead of a wheel, but they simply don't allow you to make the delicate adjustments necessary to focus well. You need a focus wheel that will move from the closest to the farthest focus with one or two revolutions. Finally, there are zoom binoculars that don't have a fixed magnification and allow you to change the magnification to focus in on an object. But you pay for this with poor optical quality, greater weight, and higher cost.

Quality instruments are of two designs: porro and roof. On classic porro binoculars, the *eyepieces,* the lenses close to your eyes, are not in line with the *objectives,* the large lenses at the front of the instrument through which light enters. One of the basic optical problems in designing binoculars is that light passing through a lens creates an inverted image. In the mid-19th century, an Italian, Ignazio Porro, invented binoculars that present an upright image by using two identical prisms in each barrel of the binocular, at right angles to each other. Each prism reflects and reverses the light, one top to bottom and the other left to right, thus presenting a proper, natural perspective to our eyes. These prisms give the binoculars their odd shape. Roof prisms were invented about the same time by the German physicist Carl Zeiss. Ernst Abbe, a professor of physics at the University of Jena, had formulated the basic mathematical laws for the paths of light. Abbe became director of research for Zeiss, and using much-improved optical glass, whose invention he had collaborated on, he created the Abbe roof prism, which conducts the light through a complicated pathway to produce an upright image. Modern roof-prism binoculars have a sleeker, more compact design, with the eyepieces and objectives in line. Neither design, however, has a performance advantage over the other. In general, porro prisms are less expensive, but they are somewhat harder to hold steady. Also, roof-prisms are less susceptible than porro-prism binoculars to becoming misaligned if dropped.

THE MEANING OF NUMBERS SUCH AS 7×35. All binoculars are designated by a pair of numbers like this. The first number, 7, is the magnification (or power). The second, 35, is the *aperture,* the diameter in millimeters of the objective lens. A magnification of 7 means the object in view appears 7 times closer. People often look only at 10× binoculars, or even higher power, assuming that greater magnification is the most important factor. But it isn't. A bird 300 feet away obviously looks tiny. With 7× binoculars, the bird appears to be only 43 feet away, clearly much better. But 8× binoculars bring it only to 37 feet and 10× to 30 feet; these are improvements over 7×, but perhaps not great enough improvements to outweigh issues of brightness and lens quality that may be much more important. Furthermore, you must be able to hold the binoculars steady, and the more the instrument magnifies an object, the more it also magnifies the slight movements of your hands. Higher-power binoculars are also heavier, making them harder to hold up and more tiring to carry. For these reasons, birders generally choose 7× or 8×.

BRIGHTNESS. Both the power of a binocular and the diameter of the objective lens determine its relative brightness. Brightness is inversely proportional to the square of the power: doubling the power reduces brightness to a fourth. The *exit pupil* of the instrument — that is, the size of the effective hole through which the light exits the binoculars and enters your eye — is the size of the objective lens size divided by the magnification — thus, 35 mm/7 = 5 mm. Other factors being equal, the larger the exit pupil, the brighter and more useful the instrument. The *brightness index* of a binocular is the square of the exit pupil diameter, so a 7×42 binocular with an exit pupil of 6 mm has a brightness index of 36, while an 8×40 binocular with an exit pupil of 5 mm has a brightness index of only 25. But optical instruments cease to be brighter when the exit pupil exceeds the pupil of your eye, which changes with the ambient light as the eye's iris expands and contracts. In bright sunlight, your iris contracts to about 2 mm; in dim light, it expands to about 7 mm. As you age, however, your pupil dilates less, so by age 40 it is limited to a maximum of about 5 mm. If you are over 40, buying binoculars with a larger exit pupil may be a waste of money. On the other hand, birders who go out on pelagic trips to see oceanic birds find that their binoculars move around a lot with respect to their eyes, especially if they wear eyeglasses. An oversize exit pupil helps keep a bird in view as you bounce around on the tossing deck with the binoculars in one hand and the other hand holding on to the boat.

FIELD OF VIEW. Another important factor in choosing binoculars is their field of view (FOV), the horizontal span you can see. Binoculars are commonly advertised as having an FOV of so many feet in view at 1,000 yards (or so many meters at 1,000 meters), or as an angle, the portion of a circle (360 degrees) that is visible, typically between 5 degrees and 8.5 degrees. A wide FOV is important in birding, and some binoculars are made with an especially wide angle. Try to find binoculars with a minimum FOV of 330 feet, and if you can find some with other desirable features that reach 400 feet or even more, so much the better. FOV may not matter much if you are watching birds at a distance, but if you are watching birds nearby as they move quickly and rather furtively through the foliage of trees, seeing a wide area at one time can make the difference between locating a bird and missing it. Lower power provides a wider field of view, so you may pay for a wide FOV with lower magnification.

DEPTH OF FIELD. When you focus your binoculars on an object, you are focused on a little slice of the world perpendicular to your line of sight, and that slice has some depth. That is, everything within the slice is essentially in focus at one time. Your binoculars should have enough depth of field — that is, the slice should be thick enough — so an entire small bird, for instance, is in focus at one time. If it isn't, you'll have to keep making fine adjustments to the focus as the bird moves a little and as you want to see its parts. As explained in chapter 11, you can also use binoculars with a good depth of field to pick out a bird in a bush that's largely surrounded by branches and leaves; you set your binoculars so the bird is inside that slice and objects that are closer or farther away are out of focus, and then you ignore everything but the bird.

TRYING THEM OUT. With all these factors in mind, you can go shopping, either in a store or with a reputable mail-order dealer that will allow you to return binoculars within a reasonable time with no penalty. When you first handle a pair of binoculars, you have three general questions to ask yourself. First, can you get your fingers around the binoculars comfortably and easily reach the focus wheel? If you can't do this, reject them immediately. Second, can you adjust the binoculars for the correct *interpupillary distance*, the distance between your eyes? You do this by rotating the binocular halves around the center hinge until you are looking comfortably *directly down each barrel.* You must be able to see a single round field instead of two separate circles of light, and you must not have a sensation of the walls of the binoculars moving into your field of view — so-called black flashes. Third, are you comfortable with their weight? Good binoculars weigh about two pounds, give or take a few ounces, and you have to feel comfortable carrying them for hours at a time. So consider the strength of your arms and shoulders, and whether you are going to get tired easily and have trouble holding the glasses up, thus taking the fun out of birding. Weight is an especially important consideration for people with back problems, who often have to seek light binoculars. You can reduce the problem by buying a harness system that takes the stress off your neck and back by distributing the weight more broadly over your shoulders; even wide, spongy straps can ease the tension. But weight is always a consideration.

While you're checking these points, make sure you can easily pull the lens caps away from the eyepieces when you want to look at something but that they remain attached to the straps and fall into place over the eyepieces when you aren't using the instrument.

If the binoculars pass these tests, you have to adjust them for your eyes to make sure you can see well with them. First, get the proper interpupillary distance. Your eyes undoubtedly differ slightly in their focus, and you compensate for this by using the *diopter adjustment* built into one eyepiece, generally the right one. Chapter 11 explains how to do this precisely when you have the time. In a store, you can do it quickly, to make the instrument good enough for further testing. First *use your left eye alone* to focus on some object several feet away with the focus wheel. Then look at the same object *with your right eye alone* and use the diopter adjustment to bring the object into focus without changing the focus wheel.

When you can see objects in focus with both eyes together, look at various things, in various lights, to test the instrument's quality. Once the power and aperture (such as 8×42) are fixed, both the exit pupil diameter and depth of field are fixed, so the most expensive pair of that type will have the same value as an inexpensive pair. Other factors are then the consequence of good design, such as long eye relief, as described below. One undesirable characteristic to screen for is uneven focus across the binocular field, so when the center of the field is focused on something the edges are slightly out of focus, and vice versa. Excellent binoculars won't show this. You should also be aware of *chromatic aberration* in some binoculars; since light of each color has a different wavelength, it will travel a slightly different path through the optics, and in a poor binocular an object may seem to have a little rainbow attached.

EYE RELIEF. The light coming through your binoculars emerges at the eyepiece and creates a sharp image at the *focal plane* of the binoculars. The distance between the ocular lens and the focal plane is the *eye relief* of the binoculars. You need a reasonable amount of eye relief to keep the instrument at a comfortable distance from your eyes. If the eye relief is too high, you'll feel as though you need to hold the binoculars too far away. You can tell if a pair of binoculars has adequate eye relief by looking through them. Binoculars with improper eye relief will give you the sensation of not being able to look straight down the barrels to get a comfortable, single, round image. If you don't wear glasses, you'll probably have the proper eye relief if you have the eyecups extended, or with a little adjustment of the eyecups. Then you should be able to look through the binoculars comfortably, and your eyes should be in a position that gives you the maximum FOV. If, however, you wear eyeglasses, eye relief becomes critical because you have to get binoculars with long enough eye relief so you can get your eyeglass lenses between the oculars and your eyes. If the eye relief values for binoculars are provided, you can look at models with larger numbers. The ABA sales catalog is good about listing eye relief figures for most binoculars, but generally you'll know if a pair is suitable only by trying them.

High eye relief designs are usually more expensive. Also, higher magnification generally means less eye relief. Many eyepieces in wide-angle binoculars have low eye relief because of their design, something to test if you are considering buying a wide-angle binocular.

THE IMPORTANCE OF CLOSE-FOCUS. Binoculars with close-focus are essential for woodland birding. Several problematic pairs of small birds are visually distinguishable only at close range. A close-focus range of 15–18 feet is the least you should accept, and for picking out the field marks on some small birds you'll be better off with a minimum range of about 10 feet. Depending on your eyes, you can find binoculars with close-focus ranges down to 6 feet. Lower-power binoculars generally have closer focus.

While in a store shopping for binoculars, you can easily determine how closely a pair of binoculars will focus. Make sure the diopter adjustment is set so objects at a comfortable distance (say, 20 to 30 feet) are in focus for both eyes. Then focus on some nearby object that you can walk toward, and get as close to it as you can while still keeping it in focus. Measure the distance to the object by counting your paces as you walk to it or with a measure such as counting floor tiles that may be a foot in width.

A WORD ABOUT SPOTTING SCOPES. When you start to associate with experienced birders, you'll see that many of them are carrying spotting scopes, telescopes that are generally mounted on tripods for viewing distant birds. If you get very serious about birding, you'll probably want one. Good spotting scopes are expensive, and they need to be mounted on strong tripods, which are also expensive. The best scopes are made by the manufacturers of the best binoculars. Each brand has its champions, and the arguments among them can be heated. Your best bet is to associate with people who have different models, test them in the field, and eventually choose your favorite. But save your money for a while.

Bibliography

I. Books Cited in the Text

Edwards, Betty. 1989. *Drawing on the Right Side of the Brain.* New York: Tarcher/Putnam.

Goodfield, June. 1981. *An Imagined World: A Story of Scientific Discovery.* New York: Harper and Row.

Hanson, Norwood Russell. 1969. *Perception and Discovery: An Introduction to Scientific Inquiry.* San Francisco: Freeman, Cooper, and Co.

Kaufman, Kenn. 1996. *Lives of North American Birds.* Boston: Houghton Mifflin.

———. 1990. *Peterson Field Guide to Advanced Birding.* Boston: Houghton Mifflin.

Pranty, Bill. 1996. *A Birder's Guide to Florida.* Colorado Springs, CO: American Birding Association.

White, Mel, and Paul Lehman. 2006. *National Geographic Guide to Birding Hotspots.* Washington, DC: National Geographic Society.

II. Field Guides and Related Resources

You'll eventually want to get some other field guides for North America, and these should top your list:

Kaufman, Kenn. 2000. *Kaufman Field Guide to Birds of North America.* Boston: Houghton Mifflin.

National Geographic Society. 2006. *Field Guide to the Birds of North America,* 5th ed. Washington, DC: National Geographic Society.

Sibley, David A. 2000. *The Sibley Guide to Birds.* New York: Knopf. Originally published as a single book and now available as separate books for eastern and western North America.

Thompson, William III, and the editors of *Bird Watcher's Digest.* 2005. *Identify Yourself: The 50 Most Common Birding Identification Challenges.* Boston: Houghton Mifflin. Valuable for examining exactly what its title says.

I strongly recommend that for birding in the West you supplement these with Kevin J. Zimmer's *The Western Bird Watcher: An Introduction to Birding in the American West* (1985, New York: Prentice-Hall), now reissued as *Birding in the American West* (2000, Ithaca, NY: Cornell University Press). Zimmer's analysis of some of the birding problems encountered in this region will cut through the difficulties.

Some other books in the Peterson Field Guide series that you will find useful as you advance are: Clark and Wheeler, *Hawks of North America*; Dunn and Garrett, *Warblers of North America*; Harrison, *Eastern Birds' Nests* and *Western Birds' Nests*; Williamson, *Hummingbirds of North America*.

To learn more about bird vocalizations and identifying birds by voice, try these books and CD sets:

Elliott, Lang, with Donald and Lillian Stokes. 1997. *Stokes Field Guide to Bird Songs.* New York: Time Warner AudioBooks.

Jellis, Rosemary. 1977. *Bird Sounds and Their Meaning.* Ithaca, NY: Cornell University Press.

Kroodsma, Donald. 2005. *The Singing Life of Birds.* Boston: Houghton Mifflin.

Stap, Don. 2005. *Birdsong.* New York: Scribner.

Walton, Richard K., and Robert W. Lawson. 1990. *Birding by Ear, Eastern/Central.* Boston: Houghton Mifflin.

———. 1990. *More Birding by Ear, Eastern/Central.* Boston: Houghton Mifflin.

———. 1990. *Western Birding by Ear.* Boston: Houghton Mifflin.

———. 1990. *More Western Birding by Ear.* Boston: Houghton Mifflin.

If you can find good copies in a used-book store, grab a classic: Richard H. Pough's *Audubon Bird Guide,* illustrated by Don Eckelberry (Garden City, NY: Doubleday and Co.). It was originally published as three separate volumes: *Small Land Birds of Eastern and Central North America,* in 1949, then *Game and Large Land Birds of Eastern and Central North America,* in 1953, and finally *Audubon Western Bird Guide,* in 1957. They were eventually combined into one book. They are superb, especially Eckelberry's paintings.

Thomas P. McElroy's *The Habitat Guide to Birding* (1974, New York: Alfred A. Knopf) takes you to various habitats and discusses the birds to be found there, adding to the theme of knowing what to expect wherever you go. John Gooders's *The Practical Ornithologist* (1990, New York: Simon and Schuster) takes much the same approach. You will also benefit from Donald and Lillian Stokes's three-volume *A Guide to Bird Behavior* (1983, Boston: Little, Brown and Co.), which discusses the behavior of several North American species in detail. Donald S. Heinzelman's *Guide to Owl Watching in North America* (1992, New York: Dover Publications) and *Guide to Hawk Watching in North America* (2004, Guilford, CT: Falcon) are obviously more specialized.

In addition to these guides, some excellent sources of basic information about all the species of North American birds are available. Three of the most useful are:

Ehrlich, Paul R., David S. Dobkin, and Darryl Wheye. 1988. *The Birder's Handbook.* New York: Simon and Schuster.

Dunne, Pete. 2006. *Pete Dunne's Essential Field Guide Companion.* Boston: Houghton Mifflin.

Two books of an encyclopedic nature are:

Leahy, Christopher. 1982. *The Birdwatcher's Companion: An Encyclopedic Handbook of North American Birdlife.* London: Robert Hale.

Terres, John K. 1991. *The Audubon Society Encyclopedia of North American Birds.* New York: Wings Books.

The classic source of information about our birds is a series of 23 volumes written and edited by Arthur Cleveland Bent, *Life Histories of North American Birds*, published between 1919 and 1968 by the Smithsonian Institution, United States National Museum, Washington, DC. The series was completed after Bent's death. The original volumes are scarce as archaeopteryx teeth, but a reprinted series issued several years ago by Dover Publications may be available from used-book dealers. Bent's series is now being supplanted by a modern series of monographs, *Birds of North America*, each about one species, written by many experts and supervised and issued by Cornell University Press. The monographs are also available online at bna.birds.cornell.edu/BNA/.

III. The Fun and Adventure of Birding and How to Do It Better

It's fun to read about people's birding adventures. One of the classics is Roger Tory Peterson's *Birds over America* (1948, New York: Dodd, Mead), supplemented by his edited *The Bird Watcher's Anthology* (1957, New York: Bonanza Books). Many of Peterson's columns from *Bird Watcher's Digest* have now been collected as *All Things Reconsidered: My Birding Adventures,* edited by Bill Thompson III (2006, Boston: Houghton Mifflin). Pete Dunne's books are always fun, and I would start with *The Feather Quest: A North American Birder's Year* (1992, New York: Dutton, Penguin Books USA). Then enjoy some of his others, including *Tales of a Low-Rent Birder* (1987, New Brunswick, NJ: Rutgers University Press) and *More Tales of a Low-Rent Birder* (1994, Austin: University of Texas Press). Try Kenn Kaufman's tale of his youthful birding adventures in *Kingbird Highway* (1997, Boston: Houghton Mifflin), subtitled *The Biggest Year in the Life of an Extreme Birder.*

Many books by nature writers record high adventure, that are not confined to birds. Try some of Edwin Way Teale's classics such as his four-volume set *North with the Spring, Journey into Summer, Autumn Across America,* and *Wandering Through Winter* (New York: Dodd, Mead, 1951–65). Others in this tradition are John Kieran's *Footnotes on Nature* (1947, Garden City, NY: Doubleday); Aldo Leopold's *A Sand County Almanac* (1949, London: Oxford University Press); Sally Carrighar's *One Day on Beetle Rock* (1945, New York: Knopf); and Franklin

Russell's *Watchers at the Pond* (1969, New York: Knopf). Look for similar books by contemporary authors, such as Roger Caras's *The Endless Migrations* (1985, New York: Dutton); Diane Ackerman's *The Moon by Whale Light* (1991, New York: Random House); and Scott Weidensaul's *Living on the Wind: Across the Hemisphere with Migratory Birds* (1999, New York: North Point Press).

Several people have written useful books about birding and how to do it better, including:

Barnes, Simon. 2004. *How to Be a (Bad) Birdwatcher.* New York: Pantheon Books.

Bernstein, Chuck. 1984. *The Joy of Birding: A Guide to Better Birdwatching.* Santa Barbara, CA: Capra Press.

Cashwell, Peter. 2003. *The Verb "to Bird": Sightings of an Avid Birder.* Philadelphia: Paul Dry Books.

Connor, Jack. 1988. *The Complete Birder: A Guide to Better Birding.* Boston: Houghton Mifflin.

Newberry, Todd, and Gene Holtan. 2005. *The Ardent Birder.* Berkeley, CA: Ten Speed Press.

Ogburn, Charlton. 1976. *The Adventure of Birds.* New York: William Morrow and Co.

Some classics that you might find in used-book stores include James Fisher's *Watching Birds* (1951, New York: Penguin Books) and Joseph J. Hickey's *A Guide to Bird Watching* (1953, Garden City, NY: Doubleday and Co.).

IV. Bird Biology, Including Special Aspects of Birds and Their Behavior

Austin, Oliver L. 1961. *Birds of the World.* New York: Golden Press.

Barnard, C. J., and D. B. A. Thompson. 1985. *Gulls and Plovers: The Ecology and Behaviour of Mixed-Species Feeding Groups.* New York: Columbia University Press.

Brooks, Bruce. 1989. *On the Wing, the Life of Birds.* New York: Charles Scribner's Sons.

Brown, Jerram L. 1987. *Helping and Communal Breeding in Birds: Ecology and Evolution.* Princeton, NJ: Princeton University Press.

Burton, Robert. 1985. *Bird Behaviour.* London: Granada Publishing Ltd.

———. 1990. *Bird Flight.* New York: Facts on File.

———. 1992. *Bird Migration: An Illustrated Account.* New York: Facts on File.

Chatterjee, Sankar. 1997. *The Rise of Birds.* Baltimore: Johns Hopkins University Press.

Colias, Nicholas E., and Elsie C. Colias. 1984. *Nest Building and Bird Behavior.* Princeton, NJ: Princeton University Press.

Dorst, Jean. 1974. *The Life of Birds* (2 vols.). New York: Columbia University Press.

Fisher, James, and Roger Tory Peterson. *The World of Birds.* Garden City, NY: Doubleday.

Gill, Frank B. 1995. *Ornithology* (2nd ed.). New York: W. H. Freeman.

Mock, Douglas W. (ed.). 1991. *Behavior and Evolution of Birds: Readings from "Scientific*

American" Magazine. New York: W. H. Freeman and Co.

Perrins, Christopher. 1976. *Birds: Their Life, Their Ways, Their World.* New York: Harry N. Abrams.

———, and Alex L. A. Middleton (eds.). 1985. *The Encyclopedia of Birds.* New York: Facts on File.

———. 1990. *The Illustrated Encyclopedia of Birds.* New York: Prentice-Hall Press.

———. 1992. *Bird Life: An Introduction to the World of Birds.* Leicester, UK: Magna Books.

Scott, Peter, and Olin S. Pettingill (eds.). 1974. *The World Atlas of Birds.* New York: Random House.

Skutch, Alexander F. 1987. *Helpers at Birds' Nests.* Iowa City: University of Iowa Press.

———. 1976. *Parent Birds and Their Young.* Austin: University of Texas Press.

Index

pelicans
    bill/food, 15, **15**, 32
    molting, 67
Perception and Discovery (Hanson), 12
perching birds. *See* Passeriformes order
permanent/fixed focus binoculars, 185
Pete Dunne on Bird Watching (Dunne), xii
Pete Dunne's Essential Field Guide Companion
        (Dunne), 78
Peterson, Roger Tory, xv
Peterson Field Guides, 5, 28, 91–92
petrels, 32
phalanges, human, 63
Phalarope
    Red, 142
    Red-necked, 142
    Wilson's, 142
phalaropes, 142
Pheasant, Ring-necked, 47, 82
Phoebes, Eastern, 173
phylum/phyla in classification, 26
Piciformes order, 35
Picoides
    pubescens, 43
    villosus, 43
Pigeon, Rock, 33, 47
pigeons
    dove vs., 33
    flight patterns, 79
Pintail, Northern, 37
pishing, 101–2
places for birding
    aquatic habitat and, 6
    criteria of, 5–6
    Gulf Coast/High Island, Texas, 83–84
    at home/neighborhood, 98
    overview, 98
    protected areas, 98
    resources on, 93–94
playing recordings while birding, 101, 102
Plover
    Black-bellied, **130**, 134, 178
    Golden-Plovers (American/Pacific), 134,
        178, 179
    Mountain, 141
    Piping, 133–34, 178, 179
    Semipalmated, **130**, 133, 178
    Snowy, 134, 178
    Wilson's, 134
plovers
    Charadrius, 133–34, 178
    description, 33, 131, **131**
    movements of, 131, **131**
    Pluvialis, 134–35
    taxonomy, 33

plumage
    definition, 66
    life year system of, 67
    types, 67–68
Pluvialis, 134–35
Podicipediformes order, 39, **39**
Porro, Ignazio, 185
porro prism binoculars, 185
posture. *See* shape/posture
Pranty's guide on Florida birding, 124
primaries
    anatomy, **57**, 62–63, **62**, **65**, 66
    comparison to human arm, 63
primary extension, 66
Procellariiformes order, 32
pronunciation of bird names, 43
Psittaciformes order, 33
ptarmigans, 31–32
Pyrrhuloxias, 51

quail, 31–32
quiz answers, 169–70, 173–74, 177–78
quizzes
    ducks/other water birds, 40–43
    hawks, 124–28, **124–27**
    identifying common birds, **52–55**, 75–77,
        75
    passerines, **73–74**, 75–77, **75**

rabbit/duck figure, 12, **12**
races/subspecies, 44
radius, human, 63
rails, 29, **29**, 33
rare bird alerts (RBAs), 94
rarities, 96
Raven, Common, 95
ravens, 23, 49, 167
RBAs (rare bird alerts), 94
reading
    guides/resources overview, 190–94
    importance of, 6
Redhead, 37
Red Jungle fowl of East Asia, 32
Redpoll, Common/Hoary, 95
Redstart, American, 163, 164, 172
Regulidae family, 70, **70**
remex/remiges, 62
    See also primaries; secondaries
reptiles and bird evolution, 63
resident birds/examples, 95
resolution (binoculars), 183–84
resources
    bird biology/behavior, 193–94
    birding, 93–94, 192–93
    field guides/related resources, 190–92